We Survived The Crash

Survival Stories from the Great Recession of 2008

By

David Reindel

With Steve Marsh

To order additional copies of this book, contact:
Xlibris Corporation
1-888-795-4274
www.Xlibris.com
Orders@Xlibris.com
115403

Table of Contents

FOREWORD

By Wayne Carini

Wayne Carini is the nationally known owner of legendary classic automobile brokerage F40 Motorsports, based in Portland, Connecticut. Wayne and his classic cars are featured in every episode of "Chasing Classic Cars," a hit TV series hosted by Wayne and the Discovery's Velocity Channel. My long-time friend and car-collecting mentor, Wayne also leads major fundraising efforts for the world-wide Autism Speaks Foundation. Here he shares his own, unique investment perspectives, which ironically shadow some of the insights shared by me—albeit from another world.

—Dave Reindel

Wayne Carini:

When Dave Reindel asked me to write the foreword for his new book, I couldn't believe it, but now I'm beginning to understand why: Dave is not your average financial planner, far from it. I've run into more than my share of financial planners.

Most toot their own horns and tell you why they can make you richer, faster, than the next guy. None of them will tell you how quickly they can lose your money while making commissions for themselves, because they do business in basically the same way. They take risks with your assets, with some knowing not a whole lot more than you do, when it comes to the way the market is going to turn.

I think Dave chose me to begin his new book because, first, we're friends. Second, I don't invest with him. Shocked? Don't be. Dave is the kind of guy who would NEVER push himself on anybody. Not his style. Also, he knows when to respect real expertise in any field. He knows I can do NO better than the way I invest right now, which is highly unusual for most people. I collect classic cars and I can safely say that my world is not for the amateur. I also know that what Dave does is highly specialized, and I would never doubt his expertise. His reputation demands that kind of respect.

Dave uses annuities and other types of insurance to keep people from going broke in retirement. I know he's one of the best experts anywhere when it comes to that. I also know that Dave always DOES what he says he will do. In my case, when he says he means to a buy one of my classic cars he will do just that.

As a well-known philanthropist, Dave does the same for our charitable foundation. His promises are good as gold, and for his clients, he is famous for delivering exactly as promised: safety and guaranteed income for a reliable retirement. So, if we are two different experts, coming from entirely different worlds, we share that same belief. We deliver the real thing, and we guide our customers to successful strategies.

Dave also knows that I'm an undisputed expert at what I do. For decades, I've had a real passion for buying and selling classic cars. Yes, it's a risky business. You REALLY have to know what you're doing to succeed, and it took me many, many years of trial and error before I began building my own private inventory of classic cars. Collectively, they are priceless and unlike so many cars you see at so-called "classic" car auctions, mine are extremely rare, which is part of my strategy.

My cars will always have a ready market because there will always be a solid core of truly wealthy people out there—people who have the means, the knowledge and the passion to invest in a very select few of the world's finest, classic automobiles. Like the rest of the investment world, there will always be a few who know the game and the ground rules. These are the people who will always make money on genuine upside investments. The rest—and this includes most car investors—will lose because they run on emotion, instead of numbers. They buy "old" cars that have been beautifully restored, but those old cars were originally manufactured and sold by the thousands, even hundreds of thousands. If this sounds strangely like the way most buyers play the stock market, it is, and their advisors tend to follow the same pattern. Ironically, we're all beginning to discover that the stock market is angled toward a few, highly informed investors, or investment groups, and that the rest of us play according to an increasingly sophisticated set of rules.

I know enough about what Dave does to tell you that he teaches his customers to give up running on investment emotion, forever. I also know that Dave respects me for what I do because Dave buys a car now and then from me.

In fact, you might have seen one of Dave's investments on my TV show, "Chasing Classic Cars," which runs on the Discovery's Velocity Channel.

We just finished filming our fourth season and car buffs are in for a real treat this year. We'll be showing some of the finest collector Ferraris I have ever seen, along with vintage Bentleys and other classics you have to "chase," rather than fend off from aggressive sellers.

I really got to know Dave for another reason altogether, and one that sets him apart from other collectors. Dave has a big heart for charities. For years, I've been involved with people who want to donate to my true passion in this world, people who support a world-wide organization called Autism Speaks, which was founded by former General Electric president, and one-time head of NBC, Bob Wright.

Bob and I have something in common. We have autistic children in our families. One of my daughters is autistic. Some of his grandchildren are autistic, which prompted Bob to start the foundation. We work together to collect money for research, while helping families with autistic adults and children. Bob also had the vision to gather up a lot of struggling, smaller autistic foundations into one large organization (Autism Speaks), which would make it possible to really get things in gear. Since then, our organization has been able to reach out to hundreds of thousands of autistic people in need. We've also been able to draw attention to basic facts: Autism now affects one in every 88 children at birth. For various reasons, that figure used to be one in 10,000 and I have my own theories about the rise—everything from medications allegedly affecting childhood flu inoculations to awareness among doctors and the way they've been able to diagnose autism itself. Some of those medications, by the way, allegedly contained heavy metals at one time, yet the meds had been approved by the FDA so we're unlikely to see much in the way of resolution.

Our daughter is now 22 and a terrific person but autism has affected her life, our lives, and the lives of millions of people worldwide. She was diagnosed at the age of 18 months. At 18 to 20 months she stopped talking. For our daughter, it was as if someone had hit a switch, and she started acting very strangely, as if she didn't know what we were talking about.

So autism is my real passion. I need to help find the real cause. We also need to help a world full of people struggling with autistic family members. I'm fortunate enough to own a good business and my daughter will be okay for the rest of her life. But what about the families that have no money, barely making ends meet on their own when they suddenly have an autistic child? The costs associated with autism are amazing, so the foundation helps with things like respite programs. For example, our daughter has to have a family member by her side 24 hours a day, which can be a little overwhelming. Fortunately we have family members in the area who can give my wife a little break now and then. Yet, a lot of families don't have that support, so Autism Speaks can provide day care and overnight stays.

There. I've said my piece, which is another illustration of the kind of generosity I've seen in Dave Reindel. That I'm allowed to present this information in a book about financial planning is equally amazing, but, again, that's Dave.

He has no autistic family members. He became a car-buying client of mine about three years ago when he came in and bought a Ferrari. I got to know Dave, watching him switch cars on a regular basis, but I didn't know what was coming. He knew I was involved with autism and one day he offered to donate $1,000. Then he bought another car from us, negotiated the cost down by around $5,000, and when he came in to pick up the car, he gave me a check for $5,000. You can imagine how puzzled I was. Car customers NEVER give US money. He donated the $5,000 price reduction on the car to Autism Speaks. I didn't know what to say.

When he came in again to swap cars, he gave us another check. He loves to switch cars, and I know he doesn't make money on any of them, but every time he does it, we get a check for Autism Speaks. I've begun to wonder if he trades and buys cars as an excuse to give us another check for the foundation, but I do know that there are very few people in the world like Dave Reindel. He even invited us to one of his book signings, in order to promote the foundation, offering all proceeds that day to Autism Speaks. Then he called and said the proceeds from the book signing might not be enough, so he sent us another check, this time for $4,000. I've heard that he does this for other people and organizations, too, as you will discover in this book.

Meanwhile, Dave started buying cars and selling cars, losing money here and there, but that's his passion. He would buy brand new cars, drive them for three or four months and sell them again, losing $10,000 to $15,000. So, I went to him and helped him put money into the right vintage cars, cars that wouldn't lose money. I gave him investment strategies: Put $200,000 into the right Ferrari, hang onto it for a couple of years, and after around two years it will go up. This will always happen if you buy the right cars, like art, furniture, anything collectible. If you buy a car because you like the lines, the shape, that's good, but how many did they produce? If they produced 35,000 of that model, it's probably not a good choice. I tell my clients to find something that was produced in a limited quantity—only 50 to 350—and that those will always be in demand. It's a logical way of thinking. But not all markets and investment strategies are logical, a perspective I'd like to add to Dave's book. Again, he has another kind of strategy and I hear that it has been quite successful for a lot of people.

As for an unsuccessful strategy, the collectible-Mustang craze happened 10-12 years ago when "muscle cars" became very fashionable. People who wanted them grew up in the 60s or 70s when they didn't have money. Now the same guy is making money, buys the vintage Barracuda he always wanted but pays WAY too much for one of 35,000 Barracudas made that year. Sadly enough, that guy would set the market price for the car. Before you knew it, other people were paying $350,000 for Barracudas that weren't worth nearly that much. It was a joke in the car world, a falsely created market.

Does this sound familiar? You bet it does. Before the crash and the recession, Joe Average went out and bought a stock because his neighbor bought the same shares. He knew nothing about it but, oh, his neighbor made a couple of bucks of profit and, along with a few thousand other people, falsely inflated the marketplace. I'm afraid the same thing is happening all over again in the stock market because I know the same kinds of passions run high on fear and greed in the collectible car business.

As for the guy who paid $350,000 for the Barracuda? He can't get $50,000 for the same car today. To win in this business, you really have to know what to buy, when to buy, how long to hold, and—this is big—you have to have enough money to buy the right car.

When it comes to Dave Reindel and what he does professionally, he's terrific, doing very well. Back when the stock market was really cranking away, I would read something about a stock, call my broker at the time and insist it was a great stock, ordering him to buy it for me. When the broker would recommend against the same stock, I would argue, pointing to people who had *already* made a lot of money on the stock, still wanting to buy in. I can still hear my broker recommend stocks with companies making toilet paper and soda, things people will always buy, stocks that would supposedly always be a sure bet, and slowly climb the ladder in price.

When it came to buying stock, I was the kind of investor who wanted to make money really quickly. Well, of course, I lost my shirt. While I stayed good on the safer stocks recommended by my broker at the time, I've seen similar companies tank in the past couple of years. I'm afraid it's a different kind of stock market today, running on a different kind of fuel altogether.

I still have a small portfolio of stocks and bonds, but now I mainly invest in what I know best: cars. If I have extra money, I won't go out and buy a stock, I'll buy cars, knowing that I have the knowledge to turn those cars around and make a profit.

I respect Dave Reindel because we share the same vision in different ways. You need the right kind of knowledge and you always want to have something to fall back on. I diversify quite a bit in things outside-the-box of the market today. I have some property, regular sales, an auto body shop, a restoration shop—all in the same location in Portland, Connecticut. And if one business is a little slow, another one picks up. You can't put all your eggs in one basket.

That's the way I see survival today and in the near future, at least. We're not a big turnover company, our overhead is small. We stay with what we know and avoid the mass market in luxury cars, where margins are small and people turn endless haggling into a hobby. We've done well with a special kind of niche. It's a different mindset and from what I know about Dave and his business, he stuck with his niche and his niche started taking bigger and bigger chunks of the investment market.

I'm not surprised because logic tells you to stick with what you truly know and understand. For me, classic car investments are second nature. Dave knows annuities like nobody else in the business, and for him the *right kind* of annuities are second nature—not every annuity is a great bet. Classic cars just keep on going because certain kinds of wealth are forever, but like anything else, markets change and you have to pay attention. For example, you need to look at the demographics of your buyer. The people who wanted cars from the 1920s and 1930s are now in their 80s and 90s, so those cars are still going to be popular, but a car from that era suddenly has to be a very special car.

From what I hear from Dave, annuities and other kinds of insurance products have changed radically with the demographics of a new market. Like the look of investment cars, your grandpa's annuity won't make it today. They have to have a whole new set of features. But I'll leave all that for him to explain.

Today, a collectible car has to be something that can be used, something you can drive on today's highway. Cars from the 1920s can be popular as long as they can keep up with traffic. Collectible cars from the 1960s are a lot more popular for that reason. So, Dave probably has a classic annuity or two in his garage, but I will bet that they keep on changing as we move into the future. I mean, who can predict where things will go in this economy?

You want to have an annuity that you can drive into the future of your retirement, maybe something like a classic 1926 Bentley that was awesome in its day and can keep up with traffic right now. I had a client who had a car like that. Before he passed away, he attached my business card to the title because he knew I loved that car. His son sold it to me and I will have it for the rest of my life. Like that car, there are classic products out there in every category, and some classic stocks worth holding onto. I've attached the same kind of thinking to the classic cars I know and love so well. I've even set up a trust fund for my daughter, the kind for special needs kids, which contains a number of automobiles—all good stuff. Some day when we're not around to care for her anymore, her trust fund will give her anything she wants or needs; the state will not be able to take everything she owns. To me, it's the same as putting assets into a gold trust, and it's a wonderful thing to be able to do for a child.

From here and moving forward, I think more and more people are going to see things the way Dave and I do. We see things in different ways, I admit, but annuities are different from other investments; they remind me of cars, in a way, because you can touch and hold on to them. If you keep up the maintenance of an annuity, they are never going to change the way they do what they're supposed to do: provide income. With stocks, you push a button on your computer and look at numbers, you can make lots of money but nothing is real enough to hold, and if you hold on to long, you can wind up with nothing but paper.

With a classic car, you can go out and sit in it, start it up, smell it, drive it, have fun with it, and at the end of the day, you're doing just as well with it as your portfolio would have been in the stock market, but you're enjoying it at the same time. Yet, you can't fund your classic car portfolio with bogus cars any more than you can buy a bunch of XYZ stocks, or annuities, that are worth junk. What good is that? You have to buy the best.

In my business, and in Dave's, you need either a lifetime of knowledge or a really good advisor.

***Before closing and just for fun, Wayne offers examples of "sweet spots"
in the classic car market:***

Any limited production Ferrari will always be good. Because 150 or less
were made, Ferrari 275s are probably best example of the way things can go
with the right car. When the market for the 275 was very bad in the early
1990s, they were down to $350,000. Two years before that they were up to
$1.5 million. Today, in spite of the recession and a big stock market crash,
they're back up to $1.3 million to $1.6 million.

Another example is the GTO Ferrari. They made only 36 GTOs, which
became part of racing history. The GTO Ferrari market went crazy in
the early 1990s and GTOs were up to $3 million. The market went
down for a little while but GTOs were always in the $1 million to $2
million price range, and now, today, you can't touch one for under *$30
million!*"

A vintage Bentley that cost $350,000 in 2007 was up to $750,000 in early
2011, all due to supply and demand and the fact that only 1,000 vintage
Bentleys were manufactured between 1922 and 1931. How many models
remain? Maybe 600. You need to go after quality, low production cars,
with just enough around to feed the market while leaving a hungry 10%
market share wanting more.

*   *   *

*I'd like to thank Wayne Carini for his great insights. Unlike annuity
carriers—great insurance companies with centuries-old reputations
for guaranteed reserves—when Ferrari production reaches a certain*

level, the company will shut down production to maintain market demand.

Quality annuities, and other insurance based products, create demand by sheer virtue of providing guaranteed income for life. No speculation required, just a knowledgeable advisor to select the right product. As for any product including the annuity, hordes of advisors would sell us the "wrong vehicle," as Wayne might say. It's up to the customer to learn about trustworthy advisors.

The upcoming life stories in this book will provide life illustrations from "real people" who have taken the high road. They've also discovered things you need to know about advisors and true safety in retirement.

On that note, let's get on the road to your financial survival!

—Dave Reindel

CHAPTER 1

Driven by More Than Money

Introductory Comments from David Reindel

If you have already read the foreword to this book, by my friend, car expert and renowned collector, Wayne Carini, you know that this book is not exactly the conventional tome about Wall Street stock tips or global postulations about the future of the world economy. You might even wonder why I chose an "out-of-the-box" investor like Wayne to talk about what he and I love with such a passion: collecting classic cars.

Wayne has been marching to a different financial drummer for most of his life; he knows what he's doing and nobody knows how to do it better than Wayne. He did his own thing as an investor and made it work. Unconventional as it may sound, Wayne became an absolute expert in the business of collecting classic cars. He now lives very comfortably, not only because of what he knows, but because he *loves* what he does.

I strongly relate to that, which is why Wayne and I have become friends. Although my own investment philosophies are vastly different—I have a passion for safety, safe-haven investments in certain types of annuities and guaranteed income, for example—like Wayne Carini, I know my own business better than almost anyone out there. People who work with me also know *for a fact* that my systems work; the investments I recommend have indeed saved the people you are about to meet from financial annihilation in the market crash and Great Recession of 2008. Go with Wayne when investing in collectible cars and you will benefit from a different kind of expertise. Go with my strategies for guaranteed income and get the same level of expertise in a different part of the investment world. In short, the world is full of experts. You simply must have a passion to find the one who is right for you. Believe me, when it's time for one of my clients to consult an attorney, a CPA or some other professional—some of whom you will also meet in this book—I never hesitate to put everyone together. This is because a successful retirement plan often calls for a team effort.

Ask anyone of the people in this book and they will tell you how much I love annuities, how much I *believe* in the power of good annuities, how much I truly enjoy saving retirement lifestyles for people who have been hit hard by the last recession.

Because of the success of my last book, *Don't Die Broke* (Agate Publishers, 2009), I get hundreds of calls from all over the nation from people wanting to know how to keep from going broke before they die. Some of them are financiers at the highest level. One is a prominent physicist. But so many others are just wonderful average people who have worked hard all their lives, who lost money in the last recession and are now resolved, more than ever before, to hang tight with my plan for peace of mind.

This book is about people who no longer have to worry a SINGLE SECOND about another stock market crash or global financial meltdown. They are about to tell you why, and I am one of them, which is why I've included an element about classic cars. Ironically, through the life-long application of my own, safe retirement strategies to *my own* investments, I now have the freedom to take a little "mad money" and have fun. With a solid future of guaranteed income ahead of me, I can afford to dabble in some of the things I really want to do. One of those things involves buying and selling automobiles, as a hobby. You can too, once you have safety and guaranteed income in lock-down mode for your future.

Because my friends and clients in this book have followed the basic principles I've been passionate about for more than 13 years, they can now do what *they want to do*. One of them loves to paint. She paints her house, she paints fine art pictures, she has painted a bright future for herself, but that's another story. Another one of my clients likes to dabble in the market, another owns real estate—you name it. After you learn to apply yourself to a solid system of guaranteed income, you can deal with the "investment" portion of your assets in a wide world of different ways.

I'm more about "income" than "investment," which might sound a little different, but we'll get to that in the upcoming chapters of *We Survived the Crash*. However, make no mistake, this book WILL tell you how to literally save your retirement from the ravage of market risk. Much of the telling comes from people who have known me through the years, people who have taken my advice from the beginning and prospered, and people who have taken the knowledge in my first book, *Don't Die Broke,* to heart. They accordingly live carefree, stress-free lives in retirement and here's the real point: they have all sorts of income levels in retirement. They are not just the super wealthy, and they say it better than I ever could: You *can* adjust your lifestyle and live without fear if you follow my principles. You can travel. You can do so much of what you want to do. But it all starts with a good, sound night's sleep.

I guess, after my solid reputation for insurance-based financial planning with good, reliable, consumer-friendly annuities—with low surrender fees and very decent earning potential—you could say that I specialize in providing an undisturbed night's sleep, otherwise known as *peace of mind.*

Before the ups and downs that ravaged retirement portfolios of people everywhere—not just during the last recession but through all kinds of market upheavals over the last 10 years—most people thought it was all about gambling on Wall Street, stepping up with the big guys and taking big risks. We all found out, finally, that the big guys play their own game and win, yet most of us are *not even allowed in their game.*

So my game is all about you and how you can play your own game, a game you simply cannot lose.

But first, as I did in my last book, let me tell you a bit about myself and what drives the passion and safe-haven-retirement ambition of Dave Reindel. My life didn't start with one of Wayne Carini's Ferrari F-40s in the garage, believe me. Far from it. I couldn't even afford a used bicycle at first. On the other hand, I came from a house filled with a lot of love, and I've never forgotten the people who made that house a happy home.

One reason I've included the car theme in this book is that I got the car bug from my father, Lawrence Reindel. You'll hear from him later on, too, but I want you to know that when you do, he taught me the most valuable thing in the world: how to work hard and pass my own prosperity onto others, like the autism foundation Wayne Carini has done so much to fund. I love driving great cars, sure. Cars are an enjoyment. But I am truly proud of being able to donate life-changing sums of money to people through some of the best charitable organizations in my part of the country. Beyond a good night's sleep, I get my utmost satisfaction from being able to help people in need through the Reindel Heritage Foundation, which helps to fund some 16 local charities around southeastern Connecticut. My foundation has pumped thousands of dollars into organizations helping people in need of housing and all sorts of other necessities.

My passion for charitable giving didn't just appear out of nowhere. It is an intrinsic part of who I am and where I came from, and I always hope I'll be able to pass some of the same passion on to others. You will accordingly run into people in this book who benefit from my charitable giving in *addition* to the foundations I've already mentioned.

Like many Americans, I grew up in a family of modest means. Working with cars became an issue because, when I was younger, the cars in my life didn't always work. This is when I began to visualize having a great car, an elegant, collectible car, one day.

We were on the way to church one morning when our only car broke down and left us in the snow, my mother in her one pair of good shoes and stockings, holding a flashlight while Dad probed the smoking engine. I sat inside the car and became resolved that one day I would have *many* cars, not just one, and that I would keep Mom and Dad in good working cars for the rest of their lives. So, I began to collect toy cars at first. I found scratched, beat up toy cars in thrift stores. I managed to buy a paint set and went to work, finding that with a bit of new paint and some TLC, the toy car would soon be ready for my collector's shelf.

When I was a little older, I had enough money to buy build-your-own kits of scale model cars. These were beautiful to both my eyes and my vivid imagination. I would spend days and days completing each car model to perfection, and when a model was done, I would sit in my room and gaze into it, all around it, imagining myself sitting in a real, full size model of the same car. In my imagination, I would then picture myself at the wheel, actually driving such an exquisite car. Truth be known, I never knew exactly where I would be going, other than to some fabulous place where people lived carefree lives.

So, my love of cars translated to a love of security, which became a more lasting passion, which is how I finally found the best road to financial security. And once I discovered a fabulous place called *Financial Serenity*, I became even more passionate about the idea of providing road maps to financial serenity for other people, including my parents. Today, I invite people to sit in their own private vehicle and visualize the place they would like to be in retirement, but not based on a dream. I do not promote dreams. I *provide* reality in peace of mind, which has never been about money, believe it or not. It's about having the passion to take control and really *plan* for a future you can really obtain.

My success came from that kind of passion. I don't remember working like a fiend, although I know I did. But truly, that passion drove my life until one day, I woke up in the morning and realized that I had won the game of life. And I want to pass that winning passion on to you.

Back to the car thing—which, okay, was kind of an excuse to fit great cars into a book about retirement—but one day early on in my financial career, it suddenly dawned on me that financial planners often refer to things in retirement portfolios as "investment vehicles." Vehicles indeed! And this brings up a key point, one that you will feel as you travel the pages of this book. You cannot just jump in any old investment vehicle, crank up the engine and race into the financial rat-race out there. Not unless you want to wind up in financial wreckage.

Not to overwork the metaphor, but I've known so many people—*men,* in particular—who work like mad to shop around for the best possible deal when buying a new car. They will drive from dealer to dealer, scour the internet for information, haggle, kick the tires and haggle some more. Then they'll finally take the keys from the salesman, drive home and brag *for a whole year* about the great deal they found at the dealership (or from Craig's List, etc.).

But when it comes to investing, the same guy can be an absolute push-over for an easy pitch from a local stockbroker at a cocktail party. I've seen it time and again, and you're about to read about some of the people who have shared that experience. All of whom will tell you that after struggling through the stock market year after year, watching their retirement portfolios go up and down and around and round—essentially delivering them back to their financial beginnings—they finally learned how to get off the Hard Luck Highway and park it. When I say, "It," I am referring to their retirement savings, most of which are now in safe, guaranteed income vehicles. And believe it, these are happy people.

Yet, like the rest of us, they had their trials. They learned that not all vehicles are alike. Today, when I empower a retirement plan—or salvage one, more often than not these days—every plan is different. Your vehicle must be carefully customized to fit your situation. It takes a lot of work, in most cases, and many meetings, before YOU decide what's right for you. I just work the math and pick the best, most consumer friendly insurance products available. I let you decide, and here I have to be honest. Not everyone wants to work with me, and I do not want to work with just anyone. Some people need risk, thinking they can somehow beat the risk-market insiders at their own game and win big. Maybe they can and I wish them well, but that's not what revs the engine of my overall strategy.

My strategy leads to one, and only one, ultimate solution: reliable, guaranteed income for the rest of your life. I cannot describe how truly exciting it is to watch a client's face when I show them that they will have enough money to retire, and not just in humble poverty. The people you are about to meet live very well. They worked hard and did well for themselves, only now they have discovered how to keep from becoming victims in the next crash, a crash sure to come. We can be sure of that.

You will hear them talk about how THEY did it, and what they did, because in the end, acceptance of some of my strategies became their own decision. So be it. NOW the latter can afford to do what they want.

After presenting some of these people to you, I'll take the wheel from time to time and add some recent insights, giving some other financial experts their own "air time" here and there. They will give you different insights about things you MUST have in order, along with my own strategies. I use the term "air time," by the way, because some of these experts have appeared on my weekly radio show. Titled *Don't Die Broke*, you can hear the show every Sunday morning at 10:00 am on WXLM AM 980, out of New London, Connecticut.

Woven among the people you are about to meet are some favorite experts from the show, who have made their wisdoms available in the following pages, for easy reference. You will soon see why.

Again, the "real people"—on the "reality show" presented here in black and white print—represent only a few of many success stories. They have been kind enough to share their stories in order to help you look seriously at the roadmap to guaranteed income, and the sheer ecstasy (I'm not kidding) it can provide for you and your loved ones.

After reading through their own words of wisdom, gained from hard-bought experience in the market, in some cases, I marvel at the way they've learned to keep a close eye on the center line in the road. They've all learned to avoid roadside distractions and finally head for home. So don't take my word for it, the words are theirs. They will tell you how to dump random experimentation in the investment casino and stick with something that works (then, with some money left over, they can head for the penny slots if they want; although most don't).

They include a former probate judge, a carpenter, a successful small business owner, a formerly astute market investor, an engineer, a minister, a food distributor, and there are more, all of whom will clearly illustrate that you do not have to have a PhD in finance from Wharton College to reach your retirement goals. Make no mistake, they are all bright, highly insightful people, but not all have a high-level of investment knowledge. Although some are quite savvy about the market, in the end—as we ALL know now—it made little difference when the new reality of global economics took control. This led to the current state of our economy, which some people call "The New Normal." We will talk about "the new financial normal," as well.

Either way, despite a doubtless swarm of friends and market investors offering friendly advice, they all have one thing in common: They knew when it was time to get out of the race and get a plan.

My friend and business partner Fran Tarkenton often points out that "an idiot with a plan is better off than a genius without one." Keep that in mind. Most of the people in this country who saw billions in losses from their retirement portfolios were NOT idiots. They just followed the long, and dearly held, notion that in order to retire you must keep every dime you own at risk. That kind of norm persisted for more than 50 years, supported by all the great financial newspapers and magazines and investment wizards (you know the names), and even some of the most powerful people in charge of our national treasury, AND people in charge of the greatest banks and investment funds in the world.

Idiots? Hardly. These are great people, in fact, but in the end, they are just people who failed to see the upcoming end of the road. So, the past is past. I look forward. Let's concentrate on what has increasingly been recognized as The New Normal for retirement planning. By the way, for obvious reasons some of the names of actual investors in his book have been changed to protect their identities; in this way I hope to spare them from endless reams of junk mail and telephone solicitation—all of the above to help preserve their *peace of mind*.

Thanks and best regards,

David Reindel

CHAPTER 2

11ᵗʰ Hour Miracle—Saved From the Abyss

Before I toss the keys to the following individual for a quick tour of the way he "Survived the Crash," let me tell you a little bit about him and the near-disaster we were able to avert.

His name is "Daniel" and we have become friends through the recession, but Daniel has been through quite a lot in a personal sense, having lost his wife in the past year—after nearly losing his life savings at the beginning of the recession.

I find Daniel's story remarkable because "something" told him to come and see me in mid-2008. He sensed something coming that would affect the economy but he wasn't sure what it would be. To be frank, neither did I although market volatility at the time had been troubling and the real estate industry was shaky to say the least. As Daniel and I sat in my office mulling over his financial situation, neither of us could have predicted that the world banking system would come to the brink of total collapse in the next few weeks, taking Wall Street and the U.S. job market down with it.

Very fortunately—and this is an understatement—we were able to put some things together for Daniel that would give him a last-minute reprieve from the devastation that would affect so many others in his situation, people on the brink of retirement. Daniel is now set to retire in a way that would have been impossible had he hesitated to get out of the market and give one of my safe-haven solutions a try.

At this writing Daniel is 62, recently widowed, and has two daughters and two grandchildren, aged 7 and 9.

We have a close connection because Daniel is a professional fundraiser affiliated with another of my favorite charities. It is a retirement home located in Groton, Conn, and the home has been a recipient of mine for several years. Daniel came aboard fairly recently and lives in nearby Pawcatuck, Conn. He'd been a fundraiser for his alma mater, Providence College, from 1984 to 2005.

I like his story because Daniel is like so many Americans, having worked hard and saved hard on what many a high-roller on Wall Street would consider a modest salary. When you think about Daniel's contributions to the world, including the gathering of funds for student programs and facilities for so many years, he is rich in terms of the living legacy he will leave behind, especially as he now continues his mission as a fundraiser for the elderly in need at the retirement home.

I am sure you will find what he to say most compelling.

—Dave Reindel

*   *   *

Daniel:

My job moved to Groton from Providence, RI, but I'd always lived in Pawcatuck during my career at a local college. We had moved to Groton for family reasons but I was still working for the college, where I'd been working for 21 years. It was a bit of a commute for me—about an hour each way—so I was looking for something to do that would be closer to home, primarily because my wife had become ill with CLL leukemia. In 2005, she required frequent treatments for this disease, so that was the primary motivator for my decision to change jobs.

When I started working at the retirement home, they had never had a fundraising program so I began one. Since I was off to a new start, my wife and I decided to take a fresh look at some of my retirement savings and find a financial planner.

Like a lot of people, we'd been getting those invitations in the mail that offer a free dinner if you attend a seminar. We'd gone to many. We'd heard from all sorts of people promoting themselves as "financial planners" and after four or five years, we never found anyone that we really felt we would want to do business with. Not that I'm being critical here. The ones we found were good, and they certainly seemed as if they knew what they were talking about. Some of them were younger, some just seemed to repeat what we'd already heard in other seminars. Nothing really clicked with any of them.

Not that it bothered either of us. We weren't in a real rush because we were still in our early 50s, so we felt that we still had time, a delay I wouldn't recommend knowing what I know now. But for the time being, let's just say nobody clicked in the financial services field. On the other hand, at least we were looking, unlike a lot of people we knew at the time, and part of me is thankful that we held off in our decision to go with any one planner.

I can tell you now, from direct experience, that when you want to shift the bulk of your retirement to an individual planner, or to a financial group, you really want to have that warm and fuzzy feeling about the people you will be dealing with. Again, we just never had that feeling, so we kept looking.

I know some people will relate to this story today because lots of people have learned from making fast decisions. At the same time, we *really* took a long time to make up our minds and that could have cost us, too. So I'd say you need to move slowly enough to get that warm feeling, but quickly enough to take yourself out of harm's way. You don't want to just sit and do nothing as you'll soon see.

We went to one of David's seminars and were kind of intrigued, but not sold. In fact, we would visit David's office three times between 2005 and 2008, when we would finally start working with him. In 2005, we had our first meeting with David after we went to one of his seminars. We were still not ready to pick a planner but we'd enjoyed his presentation. We particularly enjoyed the fact that David was different. I don't know how you can quantify this, but David seemed more genuine, and he certainly seemed like he knew what he was talking about.

More than that, there was something that really made him stand out from the other planners and the way almost all of them presented. You would always feel some kind of pressure somehow. With David, there was virtually no pressure at all. He stood up and talked about what he did. He talked about some of the things he recommended; he did not try to promise more detail if you went into a private meeting. If you wanted to have an appointment, fine, if not, that was fine, too. This is a small point, maybe, but from experience, it's rare and it says a lot about an advisor's confidence and experience. You can really smell hunger in some people, and that's mostly what you get.

So in 2005, we decided to meet with David Reindel and scheduled an appointment. At that point I was 58, at an age when a lot of people had been working with an advisor. Still, we talked, gave him our information but said we weren't ready to work with anyone yet. What David didn't know was that my wife and I had already made our minds up at that point, after meeting him that first time. We already knew that he was probably going to be the one to work with because we really felt comfortable with him.

Because of his expertise, and equally important, the way he seemed like a genuine person, someone you could trust, it made all the difference. He was just a one-person operation, along with his wife Janet, who did administrative work. We immediately felt that the service we would probably get from someone like David would be better, more immediate, than some others in bigger offices with lots of staff. We'd seen that, felt that, as I'm sure a lot of people have.

As for the recommendations he gave us, my wife and I were savers and this is where we're a little different than people who'd been working for big companies or major institutions. We were basically on our own. We'd saved a lot because I never worked in a job that gave me a retirement plan, not until the retirement home. To digress, I have a retirement plan with the retirement home now, but after so many years before the home, it will be a very small plan.

What I mean is that from the beginning at the college, we really had to fund our own retirements. Without much guidance, we wanted to make sure were going to have enough money if we wanted to retire at, say, 62 or 64. We wanted to do everything we could to have enough money and we wanted to have a vehicle that would guarantee us some kind of retirement. But again, we didn't really know about the kind of selection you have for that kind of thing.

My retirement plan at the college was through TIAA-CREF and I was in the CREF portion, split pretty much evenly with CREF stock and fixed vehicles with, say a 3.9% return through the TIAA portion, which was kind of like an annuity. But it didn't act like an annuity during the accumulation phase, although someone suggested that it would somehow be turned into an annuity-related vehicle later. Does this sound familiar? No, we weren't exactly sure how it worked—just that everybody else was going along with it.

In the end, I found that the TIAA-CREF program was basically a stock plan, which basically means that we were exposed to swings in the market, however conservative they might have been, or not.

Knowing this, we wanted to see what David would suggest. Unlike a lot of people in his field, David suggested several directions. Then he talked about annuities, and instead of focusing on just one annuity, he talked about several different types of annuities.

For example, I've learned through the years that with most annuities, you will eventually forfeit whatever you put into it. Meaning, you will get the return or payout for the rest of your life, but your heirs will never receive any of the funds left over after you pass away. Once you go, it reverts to whoever was holding your money for you—meaning the insurance company or annuity carrier. But David had some instruments that didn't operate that way. Although the products he suggested would be annuitized, or turned into payouts when you decided to receive them, after a period of time the principal would actually revert back to us! We would get our principal—our money—back. This is a good thing! We liked that! As of now, the earnings on our principle are still accumulating. I haven't started taking income yet. My wife passed away in 2010 so it's up to me from here.

Anyway, David had some different ideas we hadn't heard of before, as far as safe investment. At the same time, he showed us different ways we would be able to access our money after a certain period of time. We hadn't heard about much flexibility until then, which brings me to another point: If you aren't hearing about a lot of options, if you're feeling pressure from somebody to go one way with one thing—especially if the person seems impatient for you to make a decision about that one thing—it's time to find somebody else who can present other things. Not that all annuity people are one-product specialists.

David talked about different types of guaranteed income, as a lot of annuity people do, but David is a bit more discerning about the type of annuity he would present to a customer, as opposed to someone just going after a commission.

Still, we hesitated. When I look back now, the clock was ticking. In 2007, as the recession was just gathering steam, we went back one more time just to talk with David, just to make sure. Then we went to another one of his seminars, again, just to make sure. Again, we liked what we heard, and, again, we made another appointment to see him. We did that just to let him know that we were getting closer to the time when we were going to have to do something. Something told me that I really needed to do something. I had most of my retirement tied up in that TIAA-CREF group of funds. My wife had a small retirement tied up in a hospital in Westerly, Rhode Island, where she'd been working.

As 2007 went into 2008, we both sensed the need to maybe look for some safety for our money. News reports were more and more about the uncertain economy and housing prices, at a time when we were getting older and more ready to focus on a real plan. Finally, in June of 2008, we were ready to switch most of our assets from where we'd had them, and, finally, we set up a plan with David.

As serendipity would have it, that moment was right before the market crashed. By the end of June, in just a little more than three months from that point—*three* months—the entire global economy would start falling apart.

In June, 2008, David put our assets into an annuity vehicle that guaranteed a six percent annual interest rate for income purposes. Now, at that point in time, some people would complain about a six-percent annual interest rate, but within three or four months, that rate would start sounding like a dream. (Again, at that moment in June, the stock market was up around 14,000. People had been making all kinds of money on paper. People on the paper mountain weren't interested in a six percent return, were they?)

Luckily for my wife and I, we were at the right age at the right time. We were both 59 and we were finally ready to be a little more careful. We were hoping that we could retire at 62, and that one factor probably helped us decide to put our money in a safe place, but in a place that would give us some kind of earning power at the same time.

I can't tell you how glad I am that we made that decision. Within four or five months, people like us—all over the country—were losing everything they had.

Here's another thing about David: Some annuity people want you to put everything into their annuities, but not David. Once we were set up, he was okay with us having something in growth, so I do have an equity-related account today through the retirement home. It's a much smaller account but it gives me a chance for more aggressive growth, which is fine, now that the bulk of my assets are safe and secure with David.

I've even heard David favor some play in the stock market, if that's what you want, as long as essential retirement living expenses are secure. For us, the guarantee was all-important. We wanted to be able to guarantee that we would know exactly how much we would be getting in income, in retirement.

A lot of planners will tell you all sorts of things about how conservative, how relatively safe, their strategies are, but we'd heard that before. David was able to tell us *exactly* how much we would get at a certain date in our retirement, on a monthly and yearly basis.

Again, and I have to keep getting back to this, we made our decision and started making our moves with David from June into July, 2008. We could have put it off. We could have decided to go on vacation and get down to serious business in the fall. But we didn't, and the market went south beginning in September, 2008. By the end of October, it was all over. I have to share this with people because we could be sitting on top of another powder keg at any time.

(Editor's note: For example, market analysts in late February, 2011, were predicting unsettled market conditions due to rising oil prices being triggered by unrest around oil transport corridors from Egypt to Libya, some indicating that the mere hike of per barrel rates from, then, $100 a barrel, to $120 per barrel could thrust global markets into another downward spiral . . . and yet another recession, which luckily never happened. But it illustrates how suddenly we can find ourselves sitting on a potential powder keg.)

The move we made happened out of sheer luck. Over half of what I had saved in the CREF stock would have been lost—after all those years of working at the college. I'd built up a few hundred thousand dollars and I would have lost probably 50 percent of that. We saved it all by moving it to David's guaranteed program, and I call it sheer luck because no one—not one single financial wizard on Wall Street or in the banking industry—came close to anticipating what would actually happen in the next coming months. Sheer luck.

(In defense of the TIAA-CREF program, Daniel left a portion of assets in the TIAA guarantee portion of the TIAA-CREF package, which fared reasonably well through the crash.)

By October 2008, I was watching the whole financial world crash and burn. I remember calling David, saying, "I just can't believe how lucky I am." I told him it was unbelievable good fortune that I had decided to make that move. And what a comforting feeling it was. I knew someone else, a friend and co-worker at the college, who went into the same plan with (insurance/annuity carrier) Aviva—where David put my portfolio. My friend did the same exact thing at the same exact time, with a different agent and we were both saved at the 11th hour.

Of course, now people would point to the stock market today and talk about how much it has come back, but from what I can calculate, I doubt that I would have ever gained back what I would have lost. And here's the big question: What happens if another crash happens all over again? What do I mean by IF? It's only a matter of WHEN.

(As of December, 2010, the broad scope of equities markets had recovered beyond 11,000, moving beyond 12,000 by early 2011 and flirting with 13,000 by early 2012—this after collapsing below 7,000 in February/March '09. Yet, broad market statistics do not necessarily reflect gains among hundreds of individual stocks and mutual funds, many of which either ceased to exist or remained well below pre-crash levels.)

Daniel continues: I probably wouldn't have recovered all my losses had I stayed in equities. At the same time, my new portfolio through David and Aviva was steadily gaining six percent annually. You know, you give up something, you gain something. Like baseball, you swing for the home run or go for singles, but base hits can accumulate into a home run. Slow but steady.

As for a comparison of earnings between David's annuity and what I had before, all those years I was in the (safer) TIAA portion at the college, I was earning around three percent—sometimes more—instead of the 6% I get now. At TIAA, they set the interest rate and change it periodically, but it's guaranteed to go no lower than 3%, keeping with the projected rate of inflation, which may NOT be the inflation rate once we start dealing with the post-crash national debt. On the more aggressive side of the T-CREFF plan, I would have lost heavily, of course. Yet, even on the safer side, when I first started with the TIAA guarantee program, it was probably earning at 8% or 9%, but then my earnings dropped to 3%. Unfortunately, as earnings dropped on the safer side of the T-CREF plan, it acted more like the downside of an annuity—I couldn't easily transfer money out of the program without losing money to penalties.

That's part of the price you pay for having your money in a plan like that, or in an annuity. That's exactly why you have to be careful when you choose ANY annuity. You really have to have an expert like David who can show you all the available products, not just one or two that pay higher commissions to the salesperson. Then you need to have someone who very carefully shows you every last detail about the annuity. And then, you need to have a planner who will truly sit back and let YOU make your own decision. That's who David is. That's what he's all about, and it saved my retirement.

Today, my (annuity) portfolio is worth about $600,000 to $700,000, which will give me a guaranteed $37,000 annual income; the game plan is to wait until I'm 64 or 65 to start receiving payments from the annuity.

Add $18,000 to $20,000 a year from Social Security, or roughly $1,600 a month, also a little more from a couple of other accounts, then add in the $40,000 from David's guaranteed income program, and I could see $58,000 to $60,000 a year. The way I'm used to living, I can enjoy a reasonable lifestyle with that kind of income.

Not bad for someone who worked in non-profit fundraising his entire life. I think back to the 1980s, when I worked for Electric Boat and made $25,000 a year. I mean, the most I ever made was around $72,000, my current annual salary, so without all the extra expenses associated with commuting to work and so forth, $60,000 is going to be great—without having to work!

I don't even expect much change in lifestyle. I like to play golf, but not a lot. I'd like to play a little more golf, but I'm really involved in a lot of groups. I do volunteer work at a local hospital, and I'm involved with the local Chamber of Commerce in Mystic. After that, I really don't have a lot of expensive hobbies. I like walking, taking short trips, simple things, really.

What I really like is that after I pass away, my daughter and stepdaughter will see some of the principal from the annuity, instead of having to watch it all go back to the insurance company.

As for the future and getting involved in equities again, in another era I would have probably split up some money, but I've heard that equities will never be the same again, probably, because there's just so much volatility. In all aspects of economies and the world today, there are just so many factors that can move the market in a heartbeat, and in a big way. It's much more risky, even if you're diversified.

I do have a 403(b) plan, here at the retirement home, with about $90,000 in it right now, and I plan to put more money into that one; it's a moderately aggressive plan. But again, here's the real point, I now feel *comfortable* with that because that's the kind of money that I'm not really counting on.

When you really look at it, I'm still diversified by having $40,000 coming in guaranteed income and still some money in equities on the side—instead of having a portfolio working the other way around. So, no matter what happens in the market, I actually feel good about having money in equities.

I can't say that about people who have all their money exposed in risk, but I tend to be more on the conservative side because I'm 62 years old, because I'd like to think about retiring in maybe a couple of years.

Either way, through some luck and a lot of saving, I've positioned myself so that I'll be able to retire, and that was my goal from the beginning.

Summary Caution and Final Observations from investor Daniel

Looking back now, I want to be fair when talking about planners other than David Reindel. Before that, I never really had a planner who I would consult with on a regular basis, other than with the TIAA-CREF folks, who would meet with me only once a year, and that was through the company, as a group, and it was usually a brief meeting. Like a lot of people, I thought I was good to go with that. And for many, many years we probably were. Things went up and down but generally moved forward eventually, until the decade beginning around the year 2000, when market ups and downs began to accelerate.

After what we saw happen over the past 10 years, I'd say it's time everyone look for a good planner, and I would say that a lot of planners seem to know what they're talking about, but you need to look at their presentation, and then the follow-up. I went to a couple of planners in follow-up. One was really sharp, very engaging in the presentation, but when we went to the follow-up with him, he was like a totally different person. He was not as interested in what we had to say. It was almost as if it was his game. When he would get in front of a group of people he would present himself one way. Then when we went to him and spent five minutes in his office, we were totally turned off.

After attending more than a few seminars represented by planners in our area, I would have to say that we didn't think enough of them to even go to the follow-up meeting.

So here's the difference: David is such a low-key guy, no pressure, no pretension. He was very engaging and you could tell that he knew his industry inside and out. That's the key for me. You ask a question, you get an immediate, detailed answer. No running to file drawers, riffling through pages of documents to get it. No "I'll get back to you on that," which means they need to call some researcher somewhere, then call you back with answers you can get yourself on the internet. With David, it wasn't even like he had memorized anything; he wasn't reciting, he just knew his stuff. You can tell when someone is working from a scripted presentation. So, I think this is why he came off in such a genuine way—he wasn't acting. He was just this very comfortable, very genuine person, which is just as important as knowing the business, and I think anyone can get to this point when they finally, really know what they're talking about.

With David, the person we saw presenting the seminar was the same person we found when we went to see him in his office. He was just as nice, as was his wife and assistant Janet. And, again, there was no pressure, which I've mentioned before, but it's worth saying many times. If you sense pressure, something's driving the push, either lack of sales due to lack of interest in a product, or a lack of knowledge that prevents people from getting the product across to buyers. With Dave it was: "Okay, if you guys aren't ready, just come back and see me when you are." There wasn't even a push to set up a follow-up meeting, no pushy follow-up call two weeks later to see if we'd made a decision. None of that and you'll get a LOT of that from financial people. The lack of the usual push is one of the things we really liked about David.

That led to even more things with David, things you wouldn't expect. I talked to him about working for the retirement home and it turned out that he already knew the administrator. After we did business, he became involved with things here at the nursing home. Was he trying to play up to me for more business? If you look at the modest size of my retirement portfolio, that should be your answer. David is simply very generous. He gives to charity. He has worked with a lot of charities and he has his own foundation, which is another thing I like about him and Janet, so we've become very good friends.

And if you think his givings are a ploy to generate business, some high-profile community philanthropists play their giving to leverage more business, but that's not what David is about at all. He's so low key most people don't know who he is because he really doesn't blow his own horn.

I guess that's the best thing you could say about anyone who has been so successful. He gives back in such a great, low-key way, and that's impressive to me.

*   *   *

CHAPTER 3

A Word from Dave Reindel about Product Predictability

I hope you learned a few things you can use from my friend Daniel, and since he mentioned the way his annuity works, I want to interject a bit of information about annuities—annuities in plural—because there are so many different kinds these days.

Way back when, and I mean only 40 or 50 years ago, there were only a few types of annuities and they worked in much the same way. You know how some people can be. Once they get a certain impression about something, they paint everything else related to that "something" with a very broad brush.

So let's shift from Chasing Classic Cars to "Chasing Annuities." Just like buying the right kind of investment vehicle in the form of an automobile, you need to be just as picky about buying the annuity that's right for you. Sometimes the right product might be sold or produced in small quantities, just like the right classic automobile, while the massively produced (sometimes oversold) annuity owned by your neighbor may not be the best thing for you because, secretly, we all have slightly different goals we might not share at the next holiday party.

From time to time, and with MUCH less frequency since the 2008 market crash, you hear lingering criticisms about annuities in general. Such criticisms are much less frequent because millions of investors like Daniel, and other highly astute people in this book, have discovered the power of safety and guaranteed income. Not surprisingly, they have been running to annuities in droves, especially since 2008-2009, and annuity carriers have responded with more variation and consumer friendly options than ever before.

Yet, when you read something negative about an annuity, a lot of times it has to do with the Variable Annuity, which frustrates me because newspaper reporters often leave out the term "variable" when they levy their criticisms.

Now, let me be the first to say that while I came out fairly strongly against the Variable Annuity in my last book, *Don't Die Broke*, carriers have recently improved some kinds of Variables. They may have an income rider that will help protect your income with all kinds of rules, but again, with a Variable Annuity your principal can go up and down with the market. They're also noted for high fees.

Again, too many times while writing about annuities, critics tend to mish-mash all kinds of annuities together. Aside the Variable Annuity, you have Immediate Annuities that are set up to provide immediate income. Are Immediate Annuities perfect for everyone? No, of course they're not perfect for everyone.

Then you have plain, Fixed Annuities that give you a fixed rate—5% earnings for 5 years, and that's the rate. After that, we come to Index

Annuities and what I call the Hybrid Fixed Index Annuity, which is fairly new—been around 12 years—and it provides indexing mostly on the S&P with no loss if the market goes down.

But ALL of these annuities are basically contracts, and all contracts have RULES. Here's how I explain it: If you're going to invest in the market, you might go out and buy GE stock because you believe GE stock is going to grow. If you believe it's not going to grow, you're not going to buy it, right?

Well, with annuities, you get THIS, then THAT. If you do THIS then the carrier will do THAT. Some of the THAT is predicated on the THIS, and in THIS case, I'm talking about the annuity surrender period. Annuities have surrender periods and they're all over map.

First, critics love to talk about those notorious, 20-year surrender periods, which have absurdly high surrender charges, like 20 percent the first year, and so forth. As far as that kind of annuity—the notorious old 20-20—I don't think too many of them are even around anymore, and if they are, I don't use them. Second, even with the old 20-20, with most contracts you can withdraw 10 percent of what you have in the annuity every year, without paying surrender charges.

Getting away from the 20-20, with a lot of newer annuities you can be completely liquid in five years. They're all different depending on your age, your need.

But let's look at the other side of the investment coin, where a lot of annuity criticisms tend to originate: meaning people dealing exclusively in stocks, bonds and mutual funds—a fairly minimal breed these days, given the logical popularity of annuities. Take a mutual fund, for example, worth

$100,000 with full exposure to market risk. If the market goes down 15 percent one year, certainly not out of the question in an average year, and then I want to cash out of the mutual fund, it's going to be down 15 percent to $85,000, right? Yes, of course. Well, isn't that like getting hit with a 15% surrender charge?

For that reason, alone, the entire, concocted controversy around the surrender charge is ludicrous. It's just an excuse to avoid looking at something that may be good for you.

Even after losing their shirts and shoes in the last crash, or the "correction" before that, or the market "adjustment" before that, or the disastrous post 9/11 market crash before that, some people STILL have something we call "confirmation bias." This simply means that because you're biased toward something, you will only listen to information confirming your bias, which is not only true about political opinion it's true about almost everything from finances to music to collecting cars. In this context, if I am biased to believe that it's only good to have my money in the market, I will listen only to the good market news and not the bad market news.

Call it self-hypnosis, call it whatever you like, but until you escape the serious gravity-pull of confirmation bias and look at pure facts, you will always suffer from what Wayne Carini calls the "emotional" pull to bid on whatever you emotionally—not factually—want to buy, which is fine if you have money to burn in a casino. People like to gamble and if their other assets are secure, why not?

Get away from confirmation bias, look at the facts, and you will begin planning your retirement with cornerstone products like annuities. Are annuities the only way to go for safety? Not necessarily, but we'll get to that down the road.

*   *   *

CHAPTER 4

When to Mix, Match and Go a Different Route

Okay, with a lot of financial advisors you quickly get the impression that it's "my way or the highway." When it comes to addressing a highly individual situation with clear-cut need and—after the math is on the table—a few clear options, you will come to your own conclusion that one of my solutions will fit best.

I have some clients, however, that step outside the box. Because they have lots of assets and options, they will take my advice for their cornerstone portfolio, then go their own way—while checking back with me periodically about their inclination to follow new directions.

I really like the following client and good friend we'll call "Judge Ron." First, Ron is an absolute expert on probate as a former probate judge of more than 20 years. In fact, after Ron's upcoming segment of the book, we've included some of his invaluable and practical insights about probate itself, including the use of trusts and other issues.

For now, I just want to let Ron take center stage and explain how I fit into HIS investment strategies. Ron is what I consider a sophisticated investor. He has seen it all in probate court and he has always had his own eyes clearly on the road ahead.

By the way, Ron drives a nice car but we'll stay away from car analogies on this one. Ron seems to like houses, which he can afford, and other kinds of investment products. You will note, however, that he has included my annuity strategies at the core of his own, because he knows that ANYTHING can happen in the financial world.

As for Ron's personal stats, after more than 20 years on the bench, AND as a veteran C.P.A. and a veteran of the corporate scene as well, Ron began his retirement in May, 2010, when he turned 70.

He lives in Connecticut, about two miles from my Mystic office where he was a probate judge for 24 years, having won six, four-year terms. He retired, and only according to the rules of state law, on May 1, 2010, because the law requires judges to retire at age 70. As you will realize after reading this book, Ron has the same passion for probate that I have for annuities. Thus, he has become one of the most respected authorities on all things probate and beyond, including decedent estates, conservatorships, trusts, most children's matters, temporary custody, termination of parental rights, and a broad range of other duties.

I wanted to mention the information above because not all of us will necessarily want to retire at 65, or at any age, unless we HAVE TO. Then we might move onto other things. As such, I suspect we have yet to hear the last of the highly spirited voice of Judge Ron.

More on that in a moment. Take it away, Judge Ron . . .

Regards,

Dave Reindel

Judge Ron:

First I'd like to go over some of the mistakes people make in probate. I've seen it all. It's funny: Survivors will bring a will into court and ask for everything in the decedent's name, saying: "The will says this and that. Mother left me the house, but five years ago mom reserved it for life use and gave it to one of the other kids." They can't understand that their mother might have done something else with her assets without informing them.

When you deal with probate, you find that probate is only for items that are not totally owned by, say, a named beneficiary in an IRA or the named beneficiary in an insurance policy. If you put a beneficiary on a passbook, or, you put a son or daughter's name on a CD, it has nothing to do with probate court. It transfers by operation of law, and most people just don't understand that people do things in ways other than in written documents.

As for me and my retirement, I've been through a lot of phases in my life. I worked for Arthur Anderson, a CPA firm down on Wall Street, for three years in the early to mid-1960s. That's when my father-in-law came up with a local job posting from a major pharmaceutical company; they were looking for an accountant. My wife and I were living in New York when the job came up and I really wanted to stay in the city, but my wife didn't like living in the city. Then my father-in-law came up with a deal I couldn't refuse—he's Italian, by the way. He said that if I took the interview, liked the job and moved back to Connecticut, he would give us a house completely furnished, with the deed on the table the day we moved out of New York. Talk about a family conspiracy, but what a deal!

I interviewed with the pharmaceutical company and they offered me $2,000 more than I was making in New York. So, I decided to take the job because it fit my financial plan. I told my boss at the new company, right up front, that while I was 25 years old, I planned to retire at age 45. Pretty ambitious, right? Well, my boss didn't believe me, but that's what I started working for. I started investing, doubled up on my 401(k), put as much money as I could in company stock and put money into a credit union.

Then I hit 45. Did I retire? No way, but at age 45 I decided to run for probate judge. A whole year before he would retire, the previous judge of probate told me that he was going to retire. Right then, I decided to put in for the nomination from the Democratic town committee needing a new probate judge—and I got the nomination.

At almost that exact moment, my boss at the pharmaceutical company decided to retire, so I had a real decision to make. At the company, I was up for promotion and there were two candidates for the position—myself and another person—but they were in for a surprise. I walked into the interview and told the plant manager to hire *the other guy*. I told him that, even before announcing my candidacy, I was going to be elected judge of probate so he would have to hire the other guy eventually. The plant manager asked what would happen if I was to lose and I said, "I can't spell L.O.S.E., I can only spell "W.I.N." I said, "I know I'm going to win" and walked out the door. The plant manager never spoke to me again after that.

I ran for office in November, 1986, and won 66 percent of the vote. How did I do it? I ran as the hometown boy for the hometown job and I remained in that office for the next 24 years, having only one opponent during that time—I think I beat him with three to one—and I think it's because I love my town and the people in it.

Before retiring, I would walk to work every day past the post office to the courthouse, then walk home every day for lunch. Then I'd walk back from lunch and walk back home again in the evening, so all sorts of people along the way knew me and knew who I was. I walked back and forth every day for 20 years, even in the snow and rain when I would carry an umbrella. People would stop and ask if I wanted a ride. Even in bad weather I would decline and say I needed the exercise, and I would keep on walking.

As for another part of my life, I could have walked to one of our nearby casinos, I suppose. I live within a few miles from two casinos but I have never been a casino gambler. I am a trader in stock.

One of my jobs on Wall Street was to audit brokerage houses, and my first job was to reconcile 380 checking accounts. They gave me a specific amount of time for reconciliations, fund transfers and other duties, which I completed a few days prior to deadline. Around that time, I discovered that I liked the stock market and the way it worked. I learned about short sales. I learned so much I decided I was pretty good, so I started investing in the convertible bond market. But what I didn't realize was that once you get into convertible bonds, you can't get out until you reach the trading time-limit. You have to wait until the next day, and, in my situation as a trader, I found myself maybe 25 to 30 positions down the ladder. In the meantime the bonds kept dropping and I couldn't get out, so I lost $25,000, which I had to go and borrow from my father-in-law.

That was in 1964 and in that year I learned an early lesson: You don't fool around with professional people in their (*closed*) environment.

After that, I went into common stocks and started trading. I had a couple of brokers in New York who did very well for me. I stayed in that environment for around three years, but when I came back to Connecticut and started working for the drug company, I stayed with the stock market—trading, buying and selling. I was a stock picker who did alright sometimes, and sometimes not.

When I retired from the drug company, one thing the company allowed us to do was to take a lump-sum pension, which was considered a gamble, I guess, but I did that. I took all of my pension in company stock. By the way, while working for the drug company, I also had about 150 tax clients and small businesses on the side. So, along with working for the drug company from 8:00 to 4:00 every day, I would work on taxes for my tax clients after work, but that's another story.

Ultimately, because I'd been telling my clients not to have all their eggs in one basket, I sold all my company stock. But unlike that advice, I then put it all in Google at $260 to $270 a share. This was when Google was young, and I was lucky. About a year after the stock came out, it went as high as $650. Then a recession came along and the stock went all the way back into the $300s, I think. But instead of bailing out, I doubled up on my positions and soon the stock was selling for around $624 again. So,

I wound up with an IRA worth about $2.5 million, and with minimum distribution, at my age, about $80,000 a year.

Before moving forward with the next chapter of my life, know that I have two kids—a boy and girl, and five grandchildren between them—and what I've done is set up a custodial account for all of them, funded with Google and Apple, and with Berkshire Hathaway B shares. Why did I do this? Part of the reason was to inspire an interest in finance in my grandchildren. I'm glad to say that at age 9 and 10, my grandchildren go on the internet and watch their portfolios grow, which their portfolios did last year to the tune of around 20 percent. They're learning at a very early age that they have to start some investments if they're going to retire early. That's what I'm trying to teach them. As you'll see later on, I'll be teaching them other things as they grow.

I learned a similar lesson at an early age, so now I pass it on. When I was 14 years old, I made $2 an hour washing dishes working six days a week from 11:00 in the morning until 11:00 at night. After the summer was over I'd saved about $1,200 and I wanted to get paid in $1 bills so I could take them into my bedroom, throw them up in the air and watch them come down.

Then I went to my grandfather, a wonderful guy and a toolmaker. He seemed to know a lot about money and I asked him what I should do with mine. I'll never forget it: He took me over to a local savings bank, walked in, and introduced me to a tall man named Mr. Turner, who took my $1,200 and came back 15 minutes later with five slips of paper.

"What did you DO with my money?" I asked, almost shouting. He quietly said he'd bought me some stock, including General Motors, IBM, Pfizer and DOW Chemical. He said, "You hold onto these stocks until you get to your grandfather's age and you're going to have a lot of money, probably around $25,000."

I held onto that stock until my grandfather died at 94 years of age. At that time, those very same stocks were worth almost exactly $25,000 and that's how I learned what stocks could do. When I started I was only 14.

Today, if I have clients with teenagers in high school. If the kids make some money, I tell my clients to take some of the money and roll it into a Roth IRA for the kids, then replace some of the money they earned so the kids can spend some of it. Reason being, you can take the $2,000 or $3,000 they put into their kids' IRAs, at 15, 16 or 17 years of age, and let it run. Through the compounding of a good stock or mutual fund, the kids will have a lot of money by the time they're 60 or 65, especially if they keep their investments going through their high school or college years.

I wish my parents had thought of that, but then again they didn't have Roth IRAs when I was growing up. Still, after taking some calculated risks in my life and having done pretty well, I entered another phase. That's when I met Dave Reindel.

I used to hold all of the pharmaceutical company retirement seminars, some of which were held in New London for maybe 300 or 400 people. At the time, I found that top executives at the company were taking lump-sum pensions. Yet, none of the bread-and-butter people knew that. They didn't know that instead of taking monthly pensions, *they* could take a lump sum, too. They didn't know that they could take that lump sum to a financial planner and go their own way. They really didn't know that the money belonged to them.

I well remember one particular night at a company seminar when I told the crowd that they had an option to take the lump sum. I think the company vice presidents in New York weren't too happy with me, but I figured, what's good for the goose is good for the gander. So everybody started taking the lump sum. They all started going to financial planners in the area and I sent a lot of my own clients to a planner in Westerly, R.I., who became one of the largest Raymond James (brokers) in the nation. He was featured in publications like *Money Magazine* and did very well.

Then, one of my clients introduced me to David Reindel.

After all the people I'd ever met in almost every corner of the New York financial world, David was different. I went to see him with my wife and we saw that his office was a husband-and-wife operation. David is low-key and the type of financial planner I immediately recognized as being somebody I could trust to see some of my clients. I believed him when he said that if they liked him, fine. If they didn't, that would be fine, too. He assured me that they wouldn't get repeated follow-up calls. To this day, Dave won't bug them like brokers tend to do when they try to sell you something, and let me tell you, this is one thing that sets David Reindel apart.

But Dave's biggest plus is that he sells products that allow you to NEVER lose principal. That might sound interesting coming from someone like me, who has gone for risk many times. But it's more important than ever to know that you will never lose any money with David. Most of my (tax accounting) clients are at an age where they have a sum of money, maybe $800,000 to $2 million, and this is the last ticket on the train. They don't want to lose it, period. I send those people over to Dave.

So, yes, I've been a market player all my life, but now we have annuities, which have come from different sources.

I've also taken back first mortgages on some real estate. When my wife and I were young we invested in property. For example, when we were first married and my father-in-law gave us the house, we used to ride down to a place in Rhode Island where we saw a wonderful house on a hill. My wife loved the house and wished that we could move there when the kids were grown, so I promised that when the house came up for sale, I would buy it for her.

Wouldn't you know it? Right in the middle of tax season two years later, our dream house was up for sale and my wife wanted me to buy it. So, I called up the broker and asked about the price; they wanted $97,000 for an 11-room house on five acres of land. It was a beautiful house. The former owners were getting a divorce and wanted to get out, so I thought I'd bid $75,000 and see if they would take it.

They did. I put the house under contract for $75,000, and from there I went to the bank and told them that I owned another house down on the beach, which was then worth around $32,000 to $35,000. I told them that I would like to pledge the beach house, then told them about my company salary and about my extra income from my tax business. At that time, between the company and my tax business, I was making $15,000 to $25,000 a year, which was pretty good back in the '60s, so we took the loan. Between the mortgage principal, taxes and insurance, the mortgage payment on the house was $360 a month including tax—a pretty big sum at the time, but we didn't stop there.

My wife was in nursing school and working at a hospital in Bridgeport, Connecticut, so she had an income, too. But every time we wanted to do some investing, my wife would go out and more tax clients for me. In this way, we could keep investing in real estate, which led us to a piece of vacant property next door to our dream house. Before long, I called the property owner, who lived in New York, and found that she was asking $25,000 for the vacant property.

My strategy might sound different from others, but I offered the asking price because I've learned that if I offer, say, $22,500, and they *decline*, the next time you offer, the price could go up to $30,000. In that situation, if you try to raise your original offer back to the original asking price of $25,000, they may dig in their heels and want $35,000 the next time around. In that market, I learned the hard way to just pay the price and not to worry about it, because the price I paid would eventually rise again and again.

Yet, here's another twist to human nature. Sure enough, when I offered what she was asking, she balked, noting that the sale would mean she would owe a lot in taxes. She was having second thoughts and I could sense another rise in price, maybe because I'd accepted her offer too quickly, I don't know. I had to think fast and put my accounting know-how to work: I offered to set up a deferred sale over the next five-year period, in order to ease the tax burden. She agreed to take $2,500 down and payments of $5,000 a year for four years after that, earning 3 percent to 4 percent to help defray tax payments. We had a deal.

But we weren't done. Every time we wanted to do some investing, my wife would find me more tax clients. I was burning the candle at both ends but I had the energy, which was good because my own father called and offered to sell me HIS house. He was getting older, wanted to sell, my brother didn't want to buy it, so my wife went out and found me more tax clients and we bought THAT house.

How did we handle what could have been a touchy family situation? Here's how: We agreed to pay my father mortgage interest once a year, some of which he turned around and gifted to my brother—so he would have a legitimate share of the house, but in cash. Everybody was happy. We ended up with the house until my daughter wanted to move back to our town; when she moved back, we sold her that house.

Then my grandfather's house came up for sale and we had to find more tax clients. Now you can understand why I wound up with 150 individual tax clients and 15 small businesses. And all of this occurred while I was both a probate judge AND a practicing CPA. I would work as a probate judge from 9:00 a.m. to 4:00 p.m., go home, do some interviews, then get up at 3:00 a.m. and work from 3:00 a.m. to 8:00 a.m. on tax work, then go back to probate and work from 9:00 a.m. to 4:00 a.m., Monday through Friday. Then, I would work all day Saturday and Sunday on taxes—I did that to pay off all the investments.

Over the years we sold all the houses, other than our primary residence in town. But then it hit me. After all that hard work, maybe it was time to preserve some principal. You start looking back at everything that went in to where you are. You see the market go up and down and suddenly a person like me is ready for another kind of move.

So, I bought three or four annuities from Dave Reindel. I have a large IRA, a couple of first mortgages, insurance policies, gold coins, some silver, and we've just kind of diversified through the whole process.

My wife has two annuities and talk about a good call. She decided that, before the stock market was to take a dive in 2008, she wanted to pull out of her stock account and go into cash. There was no question about what to do with the cash. We went over to see Dave and he gave her a 10-year annuity, which matures in 2018, so it has only a few years to go (*at this printing*).

To give you an idea of how it works, she put $100,000 into two *index* annuities with Dave, which are up to $185,000 already, but that's really not biggest selling point. Mainly, you never lose your principle. If the market goes up, you share in some of the market increase. If the market goes down, you don't make any money, but you don't lose any, either.

Some people don't understand this. They can't see why they should take any money out of play in the stock market. Yet, I've heard Dave say it to so many of my clients: "Go to the casino with $100, go to the roulette table and put $100 on red or black, and if you win they'll give you 30-to-1. But if you lose, they take your $100." Now, go over to Dave's table, put it on black or red, and if you win, you get more money—not 30-to-1—but if you lose, you get your $100 back. People can understand something as simple as that: You don't lose your principal and you make money from the market.

In our situation, we are so financially set now, we have four annuities and we'll probably never take any money out because we don't need it. It's all going to be a part of our estate plan because our estate tax is on $5 million—we just about moved over that limit, but we won't have to worry about paying any estate tax for at least a couple of years.

All in all, I've made money in the market. In the crash I lost some money in the market, but I survived by staying "on it" from start to finish and I have a lot more experience than most people. Yet, no matter what happens, we'll always have the annuities we bought through Dave Reindel.

Will I invest more money in the stock market? Yes. In fact, tomorrow I'll be ready to buy some $595 money calls on Google. I'll pay maybe $3,800 per call and will buy maybe 50 calls, which will give me the right to buy the Google stock at $595 at some point. Then I'll pay $38 a call, which you have to add to the $595 so you're paying $633, or $8 more than the $625 it's selling for today. But in the end, you're really paying $800 to control 100 shares of stock, rather than buy 100 shares outright. It's more of a hedge, but it's also a gamble because the stock can go down. Yet, I've done it before and that's when Google earnings went up 50 points.

(Editor's Note: Is Judge Ron more sophisticated than many? Yes. Did he buy annuities to protect against future economic change? Of course.)

Why Did Judge Ron Go With Reindel?

I went with David and his annuities for several reasons: because he was local, because my former clients told me that whatever he said was true, and because they never lost a nickel they put with him. He's more into index annuities today and he has a new one in which you put in $100,000 and get 6 percent interest a year, guaranteed—then, when you die, your beneficiaries get $100,000 guaranteed. That's a win-win situation for someone who is 75 or 80 years old and can't get more than 1 percent in a CD.

And if you don't take the interest out every year, it adds to the insurance policy. So, it goes from $106,000 to $112,000 to $118,000. Most of my clients are very happy to dump $50,000 to $150,000 to $200,000 into one of those annuities because most of my clients are very wealthy, former pharmaceutical company people. Most of my clients walked away from the company with $800,000 to $2 million and now I'm the trustee for eight multi-million-dollar trusts.

I also went with David Reindel because I find that some financial planners are not straightforward. For example, they can be in charge of an $800,000 IRA and yet they're charging three-quarters of 1 percent to put their client's money into mutual funds. They take their fee out every month and I don't like that because they're not doing anything for their services.

I also like the fact that Dave has nothing to do with stocks; he has somebody else to handle that, if that's what you want. He's an expert in insurance, annuities and preservation of income, which plays perfectly right now and will continue to do so. Most people don't understand annuities because of the old stigma of annuities being an insurance product. Some people still feel that they'll lose money if they give their money to an insurance company. This is based on the idea that if they have a car accident and die, their kids aren't going to get a dime. And that's not the case: People need to know about products like index annuities, for example, and what they can do.

We also need to look at safe-principle products like annuities for younger people. They need to realize that Social Security is probably not going to be there when their time comes. And have we seen the last of the recessions? No. Wait until commercial mortgages start to fail.

As for us and people in our situation, our annuities will be left in trust for our grandchildren. We have five very young grandchildren and the annuities are going to be the basis for their educations. I'm 70, my wife is 65. When our grandchildren get ready to go to school, we're probably going to take some money out of the annuities because you have to remember the gift tax. Yet, there are other strategies. For example, if my grandchildren go to a particular college or university, I can take money out of the annuity and give it directly to the university without paying any gift tax.

However, what we call the $13,000 Rule is not applicable using the annuity. Under the rule, I can give anyone $13,000 a year, or jointly give a husband and wife $26,000, without paying gift tax. And if you want to take money out for educational or medical purposes, there is no limit: Here again, I can take $70,000 out of a Money Market account and give it to one of the universities for one of the grandchildren without paying a gift tax. Nor is it taxable to the grandchild, and it would not be part of the $5 million out of my lifetime exemption.

As for withdrawals from the annuity, with the annuities Dave sells, I can take out 10 percent a year without any penalty. But most likely, after the 10 years go by for the 10-year annuities, we'll roll them again because we don't need the money. Either way, we'll do whatever Dave suggests because he's the annuity professional. I know a little bit about taxes and probate, but when it comes to annuities, he's the one who knows what to do and what not to do. This is why he does a yearly review of all my clients' portfolios. He also feels that if a product is set to change, if something about any product is not going to be 100 percent true in the future (such as earnings caps or guarantees), I know he will tell them to get out of that particular product.

And here's something else that is historically different about Dave, versus other annuity advisors: If Dave advises my clients to get out of an annuity product, my clients won't pay penalties because it is possible for them to get an up-charge on a new product. He did that for a couple of my clients this year. He also sees that they get a bonus on the other end so any charges are negated, which allows for what the client ordered originally.

A lot of my clients don't even know what they have. In some cases, I took them over to Dave, who did a 1035 tax-free exchange and got them out of something that wasn't making any money; from there, he put them into something that did very, very well.

That's what happens with Dave, and that's the sort of thing that builds a great reputation. It's not just about making commissions, it's about really helping people. You have Client A, who Dave has done very well for, and Client A tells someone at a cocktail party and they call me up and ask if I know something about Dave Reindel. I can safely say that he has served many of my clients well, and that is exactly how his business has grown. That's why Dave is so well known and why he has helped people all over the country.

On that score, I'm on quite a few boards with contacts among quite a few people looking for financing ideas. They always ask me for advice and I've sent quite a few over to Dave.

Judge Ron's Faith and Final Details

In 2006, I came down with pancreatic cancer. I'm one of the 4 percent who beat it and I can't quite figure out why. I went in to ask for a Whipple treatment and the Lord was looking after me. A doctor told me to go home and get my wills and trusts together; he didn't think I was going to make it, but I demanded to use a certain doctor, who was booked. In spite of that, I went for the pre-op anyway, hoping someone would cancel. Someone did, I got the operation before the cancer spread and I am now cancer-free. As for health care, another tricky area, I had good coverage from the State of Connecticut; health care is another area where gambling is completely inappropriate.

Whatever you do in life—and I've taken some gambles—I also believe that you have to have some faith. A friend of mine flew to Italy when he found he had cancer and prayed on an Italian mountain top. I had a former client into health healing who prayed for him twice a month and the man with cancer credits God and prayer more than anything for his healing.

Another area in need of coverage is disability insurance, especially for sole proprietors: I had a doctor client in New London who had a very good practice, making $280,000 a year. He had disability insurance through his business but he would always argue with me about having to pay taxes on his disability. I told him that if he ever had to collect, it would be tax free. Five years later, he became disabled and he now gets $10,000 a month through disability. Tax free!

Beyond that, I always tell my clients to pay themselves first. Whatever you make, you have to take a certain percentage and do something with it for your retirement. If you make a dollar, take the first 10 or 15 cents and set it aside. Put it into an annuity, put it into stocks, but pay yourself first.

Taking risk depends on the individual. Some risk the stock market, others are so conservative all they want to do is put money into CDs and cash. But for the conservative, CDs and cash aren't going to help them in the long run; they need to put the money into an annuity.

As for risk tolerance, markets go up and down. Back in 1978, when I was with the pharmaceutical company, the market took a big drop and my boss' wife forced him to sell all of his company stock. It caused a big tax problem for him but she was afraid that the world was coming to an end. After 1978, the company stock went up again. After two splits, it went from the mid-$30s to $150—a three-for-one gain. Instead of having a $1.5 million estate, he could have had a $10 million or $12 million estate.

What I'm saying is that if you play the market, you cannot play with emotion or it will kill you every time. Whether or not you can play the market, with or without emotion, you need to have something in a safe haven. I can say that now and still play the market because we have enough saved in annuities. Now, today, putting my extra money in the market is more like a game and if I win the game, I can do more for people before I leave this earth.

But buy and hold is not the way to go, either. These days, if you play the market, I believe you need to have four or five stocks which you will have to look at and track on a regular basis. If you have confidence in them, you buy. If you don't, you have to sell. Either way, you have to pay a lot more attention to your situation these days, and you still need safe-haven, gold coins in a safe deposit box, and annuities just in case everything goes to hell. Again, take a good look at Dave's annuities. They are not your grandmother's annuities. They do a lot more and they will save you from the next crash.

Now, all I have to do is learn to be retired. My wife, Kathleen, and I stay at home a lot. We go to the movies and out to restaurants. We go to Florida for two weeks every year, but mostly we stay at home with our grandchildren. I still help people with taxes but I gave up my C.P.A. license. Yet, I still can't get probate out of my system. The local probate judge has had health problems so I've been handling some administrative problems, helping with the merger of three courts into one, which is now centered in nearby Groton, Connecticut. While trying to set up the court, I've been probating on the side. You could say I'm a workaholic but, really, I just like to stay in the game.

CHAPTER 5

How "Boring" Documents Prevent Probate Horrors

Let me tell you about "boring" documents and the pending drama you might find in probate court.

If you want to put yourself on the center stage of a real horror show, just do what too many people do: Avoid those "boring" legal documents that can save you from probate nightmares, because if you do, nightmares are what you will almost assuredly get.

I've spent many hours helping clients try to disentangle themselves from the kind of legal quagmire only probate can offer. For this reason, alone, I've met many of the good people who work in probate, and they are good people. They face procrastinators every day who blow up in fury at probate workers, judges and lawyers because they go through life refusing to take responsibility for their own family affairs.

I hate to say that, I really do, but it's a sad fact, and you will be your own worst enemy if you fail to heed the incredibly valuable, solid gold advice of my good friend and following guest, Meredith

Russell, for 21 years a lawyer who has made a specialty of helping people through our regional probate system in and around the State of Connecticut. She is well known around New London County for handling estate matters, and is often asked by probate to help handle matters in all sorts of situations.

Additional comments from former probate Judge Ron follow what Meredith has to say. Both offer vitally important insights based on years of experience.

While some of the fine print in the Connecticut probate system might differ from rules and protocol in your state, you can be sure that the following issues and elements would almost certainly apply to your local probate system. I said "almost" certainly. Aha, I give myself a little loophole, here. Since we're dealing with lawyers, why not? And lawyers are the ones you need to deal with in your state when preparing to AVOID probate. So those little differences can become major stumbling blocks without a lawyer trained to deal with probate in YOUR area. Get one. That's the best advice I can give, based on much experience.

As for the discount route and as many a TV daredevil has said through the years, "don't try this at home" with a handful of do-it-yourself bookstore legal documents. I've seen and heard for myself the tribulations of many a tongue-tied victim of sketchy legal documentation as he or she stumbles through probate, due to wills crafted by some family member with a gift for words but no probate legal experience.

Problems occur when people think, "Oh, I don't have that many assets to worry about, so I'll just leave it all to my kids after I die."

If you have that kind of non-plan in mind, prepare for the fact that your survivors may never see a dime or the key to the home you want them to have when you pass on, and what about before you die? Did you know that your estate can hang in limbo with funds inaccessible to your spouse for months or years in certain situations, as you languish in hospice, a hospital, or a nursing home?

Guess where your spouse and children wind up in that situation? Standing for days, months or even years in front of probate magistrates, that's where, and this is exactly where many families wind up in terrible feuds.

For the reasons stated above and so many more, what you are about to read may be the most important jewels of wisdom you will ever know. After you read them, get a lawyer to help you follow through. It won't take long and the money you spend will potentially save you thousands into the hundreds of thousands of dollars, along with dozens to hundreds of hours of frustration. It might even save your home from liquidation.

The following segment of the book comes in a Question/Answer format, which occurred as I recently interviewed Meredith.

Meanwhile, I want to thank Meredith for kindly sharing this introductory information. Thank yourself for taking her advice to heart for the loved ones you leave behind.

Most Sincerely,

David Reindel

Meredith Russell:

When most people think of estate planning, they think of the preparations of a last will and testament, which is the document by which the assets you own at time of death are passed on to people in your will. But estate planning has many components that involve care and decision-making involving your body during life, and during terminal illness.

Trust instruments are also used to pass assets to the next generation upon death. My view of estate planning involves planning today for the events that may happen while you're still alive. Estate planning goes beyond wills or trusts.

Reindel: What I see a lot of times are people who go from "I'm okay" to "I'm dead." But what if I'm incapacitated? What if I can't make decisions? What do we need to cover the holes and continuums?

It's never too soon to be consulting an attorney about not only your will, or a trust, which will pass what's left upon your death, but to plan for the event of your becoming incapacitated by a major illness, by a car accident, by a stroke or one of the dementias, where you can't handle your affairs.

Who will make the decisions then, not only about the use and management of your assets, but also the decisions regarding your medical care, nursing home care, at-home long term care? Those are all the types of things an attorney—who does what I do—gets involved with, and the sooner the better.

In addition to your will or possibly a trust, to cover the gap between life and death and when you need certain things, you will be talking to an attorney about establishing a "power of attorney"—you will need to appoint somebody who will manage your assets or handle your financial affairs, in the event that you are unable to do so.

The inability may be permanent or it may be temporary—like overcoming a massive car accident or a heart attack. In addition to power of attorney, you would appoint a health care representative and appoint a conservator. This is a document by which your representative will be empowered to talk with your doctors, make medical decisions, evaluate—based on what doctors are saying—what course of treatment you should have or should not have. So if you become incapable, this person can decide if a nursing home is appropriate, or he or she can arrange for in-home care.

The third document is colloquially called "the living will." This is a directive to any medical provider. It's made while you are of sound mind and says how much or how little extreme medical measures you wish to have taken, in the event that you become terminally ill.

Those are the three basics: durable power of attorney, the appointment of a health care representative, and the living will, that I consider to be part of estate planning.

Reindel: These are important documents, but what if I don't have them? Won't the state take over? What happens?

These are documents by which you exercise control over yourself. If you do not have these documents in place and something happens, then your family is going to have to go to the probate court and say, "We need to have a conservatorship; he's had a major accident; who is going to make decisions about paying the bills and collecting his income and deciding what the course of a doctor's treatment will be?"

I was appointed attorney for a young woman in her early 40s, a single mother with a 14-year-old child and a house. She was in a single car accident, she was in a coma and rushed to Yale-Newhaven hospital, which is where I met with her and, of course, could not communicate with her.

Her widowed mother had to approach the probate court and asked to be appointed conservator of her daughter's affairs because there was nobody in place to do those things. The young woman was at Yale-Newhaven hospital for 3-1/2 months and she was at Gaylord Hospital for five months, at a time when her mother was very, very concerned about whether her daughter would survive this horrific accident.

The mother was also concerned about helping her 14-year-old grandson get through the trauma of his mother's horrific accident. Yet she had to go through probate court, meet with a stranger—that would be me—and try to figure out what to do next.

If her daughter had had the appropriate documents in place, which I've described, probate court would not have been necessary because somebody—possibly the mother, or best friend, or former husband—would have been appointed by these documents, would have been able to step in and handle the financial affairs, would have been able to meet with the doctors to discuss what should be done, and what should not be done.

You don't want to be making these kinds of decisions on top of the ones that have to be made at a time when you are already under tremendous stress.

*   *   *

And now, former probate Judge Ron adds additionally valuable advice.

Judge Ron:

It's a plain statistical fact that 45 percent of the people in the State of Connecticut do not have a will. Forty-Five percent! Do they have it on paper? No, they have it in their MIND. So if you don't take care of your situation, the state will tell you where the assets are supposed to go to. And do they go where you want them to go? Not necessarily.

One of things I keep telling my clients, due to changes in the state probate system in Connecticut: You really need a trust, and you need a power of attorney. Let me give you an example. I know of a woman who was going to a New York attorney to have her will put together. It was 46 to 48 pages long. A lot of boilerplate stuff. When I did a little consultation with her she said she had her home in Connecticut. She had a condo in NY, an apartment in Washington, DC, and she had a brokerage account somewhere else.

I asked: "By the way, who is the executor of the will?" She said her attorney was the executor. I said, "Well, with your estate, and his fees, because he's going to be probating in Connecticut, probating in New York, and probating in Washington, DC, you will have given him his retirement package. You can expect your heirs to be spending at least $250,000 in legal fees."

For her, my suggestion was to do an inter-vivo trust, or a living trust, placing the property in Connecticut, in New York and in Washington, DC, and the brokerage account, under her social security number. I told her to keep it under her own control until her eyes closed, until the successor's trustee takes over, in order to avoid all the probating.

Most likely, once her estate is settled with the successor's trustee, the fee might be $10,000 or $12,000. I had her compare that to the $250,000 fee and she was amazed. She said, "Well, maybe that's why the attorney wanted me to have a will."

"That is most likely," I said, "because he wanted to have his retirement." We hear this all the time. People just don't want to do what they need to do with trusts and documents. I think people are afraid to admit that ultimately they're going to die, so they avoid taking care of related issues.

Here's the point I've been trying to make for the last 27 years: You have a will, and let's assume you want the house to go, say, to the three kids equally. Well, during your lifetime you decide you're going to want to transfer the house to your daughter, and you figure that once you die, the house goes to the daughter, that she can sell it and split the money. Well, it doesn't happen like that because this situation will not go through probate. It's not a joint bank account, it's not a situation involving beneficiaries to a life insurance policy, and it won't be dealing with beneficiaries of annuities. People come in as executors with all sorts of misconceptions.

As for a trust, a trust will also let you avoid having to have a conservator. This is a big deal because when you become incapable and can't handle your own affairs, normally the trust document will give the successor-trustee the power to do what the doctor's report says, then you can move on. It's better than going into probate court, having the expenses of having an attorney, having the expense of dealing with three-year accounting every three years, having some unrelated person know exactly what and where all of your assets are. That's an advantage of a trust. It's very private. It doesn't go through probate. Nobody has to know that if you die you're leaving behind $25,000 or $25 million. Put it in probate, it's open to the public, it's open to anybody.

In other words, most people try not to go into the probate system anymore because it's getting too difficult and too expensive.

Reindel: How much money should someone have before considering a trust?

With existing laws, today, we have a $ 2 million exemption in the State of Connecticut. Up to that point you pay no tax. And we had no federal tax until Dec. 31, 2010, when the exemption went up to $5 million. So, I'd say you would need about $2 million to go through the process of forming a trust. You want to take your assets and divide them down the middle between the husband and the wife, to make sure that when the first one dies, that portion goes into trust for the benefit of the surviving spouse, and then the remaining or surviving assets ultimately go to the kids, tax free.

The alternative is probate and in the typical situation these days, thousands of people have to turn to a handful of clerks to get things through. It takes a lot of time.

Reindel: I agree. Let's say I don't have a lot of money, but let's say I have an IRA account, and I have a beneficiary and a contingent beneficiary to that account: If I have that and $200,000 in joint bank accounts and I own a house, maybe I want to have just the house in a trust. Whatever I want, here's the whole point: I need good counsel, not boilerplate trusts. My other concerns are over *power of attorneys and living probate issues. Some people don't care about their kids, preferring to let them work it out if things happen. But at the very least, I am doing a disservice to my wife if I don't have powers of attorney.*

(Editor's note: Some of the comments above include excerpts from our "Don't Die Broke" radio show, which include aired segments that may be found on our web site www.davidreindel.com)

CHAPTER 6

Out of Thin Air:
Creating a Plan without a Plan

I found Ken, or he found me, and Ken had no real plan for retirement. He'd been saving, trying to invest and make things grow in his portfolio, but after watching gains and losses run headlong into the Crash of 2008, Ken wasn't sure if he would ever be able to retire.

He is still the hard-working, self-employed representative for a high-end specialty foods wholesaler. You've seen their products all over Manhattan, where Ken does the canvassing, direct sales and delivery of goods. At one time, he had many accounts in the Twin Towers.

Now, at last and after years of hard work, Ken can see a light at the end of the road. After following my plan, he'll soon be able to leave the food industry behind and enjoy life to the fullest. Meanwhile, Ken lives in southeastern Connecticut but is on the road a lot these days, so we were fortunate enough to catch him between stops along the eastern seaboard.

One thing I can tell you is that no one will be able to yank the financial rug out from under Ken anymore. He can be sure of that.

I'm especially proud of being able to help people like Ken realize a day when they can actually, finally, put work behind them—and forget about losing everything to a risky stock market that has become more and more controlled by vast electronic trading systems and insider dealings the rest of us know nothing about. We'll talk about that later on in this book.

Other than that, I want everyone to know that putting Ken's financial situation into a safe, secure focus has been every bit as important to me as enabling the multi-million dollar retirement plans of my other clients. That's why I am especially happy to include Ken with the others.

After the last debacle on Wall Street, and after too many financial disasters well before the 2008 crash, many millions of Americans out there will agree that we all stand to learn from Ken's story of financial survival. I especially appreciate his willingness to speak out and carry on.

*With **Your** Retirement in Mind,*

Dave Reindel

*   *   *

Ken:

I stumbled onto David's Sunday morning radio show, surfing through the channels, and unlike other shows like it, I began listening to what this man had to say. I was at the point that I needed someone (new) to help me plan for retirement.

The more I listened, the more interested I got. Finally, I found myself listening to him every Sunday for a month or two before I said "I've got to call this guy."

I didn't really have a solid plan for retirement. At my age I thought I should have done something years ago, and for just as many years I thought I was doing something that would leave me in good shape in the end, but I finally realized—after so many ups and downs in the stock market—that I was getting nowhere fast.

I was investing in stocks, basically, and as everybody knows 2008 came along, and that's when everything smacked right into a stone wall. I didn't know what else to do. I held very little value for stock brokers at that point. I'd been through quite a few and found that none of them really knew how to set me up in retirement. As a matter of fact, to this day I don't know if any of them really cared about me or not. As we all know, as we move along in life we realize that a broker is really interested in two things: buying stock and selling stock for commissions.

Beyond that, I got a feeling that most of these guys really don't know what's going on with any particular stock they're trying to sell you. It's as if they're trying to find the crystal ball. And I think that at that point, before I called David Reindel, I knew there was something I was supposed to do. I just didn't know what, and I didn't know where to go. I didn't know that a person such as David Reindel could actually pick up the pieces after the crash of 2008 and point me in the right direction.

My story is fairly typical and more common than not. I first entered the stock market in my early 40s, which was around 1985. Before then, banks were paying 10 and 12 percent interest a year! That's what I was actually earning in bank accounts and money markets, which is hard to believe today, but there we were. It didn't take much to save and plan for retirement. All you had to do was work hard and count on the strength and dependability of the American economy and the way we did business.

With basic savings accounts and a little discipline, I got to $10,000 and beyond. That was my original investment. Oh, how we took everything for granted back then. Everybody had a pocketful of money and money was no object in the Reagan years. I think back to his administration and want to bless that man to this day. I still support his ranch and his youth foundation for the sheer memory of the stable economy we once had. It was unbelievable: 10 percent interest. Today you get one percent from most banks and we still had to bail them out after the 2008 crash.

Back in the beginning, when I had my first $10,000 in savings, somebody told me that if I put $2,000 a year into my IRA I'd have a million dollars by the time I wanted to retire. That sounded great to me and I was a believer. After all there were no real financial train wrecks, only short-term adjustments from time to time. Things just kept growing, so I started putting $2,000 a year into an IRA, the maximum allowed by the IRS at the time.

From there, I went into the American Family of Mutual Funds, which turned out to be a pretty decent investment. I went into American Family with around $10,000 from savings, through a particular broker, and I stayed with him several years, buying stock here and there, buying 100 shares of, say, Kodak, and I thought we would do pretty well. In fact, back then I thought maybe I was going to make a pile of money.

Looking back at the moment, I ask myself why my broker didn't put me into blue chips. In retrospect, why didn't the guy put me into General Electric, Exxon-Mobile, Coca-Cola, right off the bat? We went into Kodak, Rubbermaid and Pfizer—companies like that, and good companies at the time—but why not the really big names? I mean, Pfizer was a good, hot stock at that time, but Rubbermaid really didn't produce anything in terms of gains during the same time period. So, I initially bought 100 shares of Pfizer, then I bought another 100 shares after that, then the stock doubled.

By the mid-1990s I wound up—after transferring years of contributions from my IRA—with around $100,000 with this broker, and that was the total after all was said and done.

Then something began to go sour with this guy and I hope people can learn something from what I'm about to recount:

It was year-end and I called him up to wish him a happy holiday season. But instead of just wishing me the same, he nearly jumped down my throat, saying, "Oh, I have these two companies that you've got to get into. If you want to retire early you gotta' do this, gotta' do this, gotta' do this.

I was sitting there with my teeth in my mouth, thinking this guy knew something I didn't. He wanted me to transfer some cash, some Pfizer stock and some other shares into this hot new security. *"You gotta' do this, gotta' do it, gotta' do it."* Okay, so I trusted the guy by then and went ahead and did it.

We moved $50,000 into the two companies he was so high on. By then we were in the late 1990s. Little did I know that we were on the brink of a major crash on the S&P. That's something people today "gotta'" realize, especially younger investors. The last crash in '08 was bad, really bad, but it hasn't been the only gut wrenching drop on the DOW. From the coming late-1990s crash on the S&P—that would soon take away my $50,000—through the better part of the 2000 decade ending up in the wipe-out in October, 2008, we had many, many upsets in the stock and bond markets. This is a known fact that older guys like me remember, but I'm afraid a lot of us will soon forget about it. Soon as the market begins to top out, there we go, ready to drop back in the tank.

So there I was in the late 90s, transferring my money into a so-called red-hot tech stock. Well, guess what happened next? Within a few days or weeks, we all watched a mystery bubble in technology burst like a balloon in a lightning storm. Turns out, a lot of those stocks were based on air and a promise. I found myself trying to keep track of these two stocks, technology stocks, which were going down, down and down. This was depressing so I decided to stop watching them altogether until they came back. Big mistake.

Before I knew it, both tech stocks went down to absolutely nothing. They'd been somewhere up in the thirties when I bought them on the advice of this broker and they went all the way down to one or two dollars a share. And here's the moral of the story about "buy and hold:" I held, but those two tech stocks never came back. This is the kind of reality the brokers and stock-pumping publications never seem to talk about. You can lose it all. I did. My $50,000 was gone. It amounted to half of everything I had.

So I went to call the stock broker who had pushed the hot tip on the tech stocks. Lo and behold, I couldn't get hold of him and I'm asking myself, if this guy really knew what had been going on, why didn't he call me? Why didn't he tell me to bail before they really took a dive? I didn't know at the time but that's not the way it works. You buy, they make money and, all too often, you're on your own. Look at it this way, unless you're dealing with some rock-solid product like a good annuity, how can a stock broker maintain hundreds of client stock portfolios and keep an eye on every one at the same time? You don't need to be a genius in math to know they can't.

Now I know that I should have been watching more closely myself, but should I have known to watch for? At that point, I was so upset with this guy I'm glad I didn't run into him on the street. It wouldn't have been pretty. So, I closed my account. I pulled all my money out of there and got away from that particular broker. And if you haven't noticed, take it from me: This guy had obviously been out to boost his year-end quota of commissions when he sold me those stocks. Now I can clearly hear the way he sounded on the phone, but back then, I thought I was getting a personal stock tip, just for me. In reality, he'd been humping on the phone to everybody else, just to get his year-end commissions up at my expense, and at the expense of other people.

So much for my $50,000, which went away with the tech-stock crash around late 1999 into 2000—when everything was going down. By 2008, everybody had forgotten all about it, but that's another story. Just after losing by $50,000, I moved into another brokerage—you've heard the name all over TV—but that was a brief encounter; the guy didn't do too much for me. It was like he was kind of blasé, so there wasn't much happening for me, of course, and his company eventually closed that particular office altogether.

At that point I moved again and went to a small company here in (southeastern Connecticut), where, basically, I experienced the same treatment. They were selling stocks, buying stocks, and I didn't seem to be part of the action. There's a pattern here, right? These people really don't know what they're doing. They're selling a product, they're buying a product, they're making commissions. That's all. So it became apparent to me, kind of late in the game, that I was going nowhere fast. I saw my totals going down again, or my totals would be standing still until they'd get just enough of a jump to keep me going in the stock, which would back off again. I'm not joking when I say I felt the way you feel after playing slot machines; the system feeds out a few little jackpots, but you walk out of the casino empty-handed in the end. I said to myself, "This is not what I need; this is not helping me."

This was 2001 into 2002, around the post-9/11 crash. Forget the dive on the S&P, the post-9/11 dump really hurt. But by then, like a lot of people, I decided to let things ride because I didn't know where to go or how to improve my program and, in my opinion, neither did anybody else. So, I let it ride on the usual "buy and hold" idea that everything would bounce back. I kept adding to my savings, really trying to get things back up, hoping the market would just keep growing. By 2005 or so, I had probably accumulated somewhere around 200,000, which sounds pretty good. But after all I'd had in there over the years, it should have been much better than that.

By the way, from the early 1990s on up, I give credit for most of my gains to what I had in the American Funds. In addition, I'd bought some E-bond savings bonds on a weekly basis through a bank. Moving from 2005 through 2007, and up until recently, I made some gains after moving into a local company out of New Jersey, through a local broker in (southeastern

Connecticut). I gave him my SEP, my IRA and my existing brokerage account, and they did alright. I came out of everything I had in that company with roughly $250,000 in the American Family mutual funds being managed by the local broker, but that was the main part of every gain I'd made since 1992. Then the funds took a hit during the crash of 2008, but not as big a hit as other companies because their management team is highly skilled. American Funds is a wonderful company with a good leg up on research and I lost maybe 10 percent, at the most, through the crash. Then they made a pretty good comeback after the dust settled.

I had other investments in addition to the $250,000, but by then I came away thinking, "What now?" Do I stay in and gamble that it won't happen again? Or do I look at my age, face the facts, and cut my losses with a plan that won't let me down, no matter what?

I decided to go with David Reindel because I want to actually retire. To do so, I sold the American Investors Fund and the Washington Mutual Fund, two great funds, both growth and income funds. I hated to do it, but there still wasn't enough in the funds for me to retire on, and I didn't want to risk another slump in the economy—nor do I want to take that risk today.

By the time I got to David, when I pulled everything out, including the American Funds, I had only around $440,000 after investing for more than 25 years. If that sounds like a lot, remember how I'd been told I'd have $1 million by now, if I'd stayed the course. For me, it was time to get off the roller coaster.

When I went to David, he put the $440,000 into three different annuity contracts: ING, with a $142,500 premium, which also includes an entry bonus. Then I went into an Allianz annuity with a $170,800 initial premium. The last one is $100,000 with American Equity, $100,000, and they're all equity index annuities. They all have incentive bonuses that could be used to offset fees, if I need to make early withdrawals according to the amount the rules allow every year.

David's plan is that I should wait at least five years before taking payments, so it's not like a 20-year stretch. I told David I'd be willing to live on $50,000 to $60,000 a year when all is said and done. I'm divorced, I have no significant bills or expenses and he felt that after five years, I'd be able to draw enough income out of these contracts and use that money, in addition to Social Security, to get where I need to be.

In addition, I now know my investments won't go down. They'll stay right where they are in terms of my initial investments. But if the stock market goes up, my earnings from these annuities will go up. And if the market goes down, I don't lose anything I've gained. Mainly, I'll never lose any of my original, principal investments in the annuities.

In my earlier days I'd hoped to be able to kick it up a little more, but I'm satisfied. I'm not looking to own four houses around the world with four Bentleys in each garage. That's not me anyway.

I asked David if I could put more money into the annuities. If he'd been like some of the brokers I've been through, he would have been too happy to sell me more annuities. But he said, "No, I'd rather see you build up your cash from this point on, and let the annuities do their thing for you." I was impressed. I've never had anybody in the financial world give me an answer like that. He was being very honest about it, which is one of so many reasons why I trust David so much. After talking to him, getting to know him, after listening to his show, he talks to me and gives me straight answers. If I was talking to a stock broker, the answer would always be to buy more stock.

What drew me to his radio show was the phrase "Don't Die Broke." It pricked my ears and then I heard he'd written a book with that title, and I really related to it. Then he started talking about the economy, what's going on in politics—a national nightmare—and he started saying things I had been thinking about, things that really affect all of us.

I think politics in general have done a number on our job market and the economy. That's what's been really hurtful to everybody. Take the globalization of the economy—the politicians seem to be drunk on globalization—who knows where it will all lead? I know one thing after years and years of experience, politicians, like stock brokers, are in it for themselves. Politicians are in it to get re-elected, otherwise, why let big companies—the same companies that fund their campaigns—send so many jobs overseas? Will the jobs ever come back? David was right on line with the way I was thinking. I heard what I'd been avoiding all those years: If things get worse before they get better—even if they do get better for a while—nowadays the only one who can lock things down with guaranteed income for me is ME.

David also adds a lot of common sense about the bailouts. Why did we bailing out General Motors? Why not let the market take its course? Let General Electric take its course. We're bailing out banks and the auto industry and bankrupting the country. Some of our bankers are the sleaziest entities on the planet. Their banks are more profitable than ever before, and we haven't seen a dime back in gratitude from them since the bailout. Just so many things done by the government have been contrary to the financial basis of this country, including Obama-care. How can any country even think about demanding that people buy a product, like health insurance, or face a fine . . . especially in a recession like the one we've been through?

Part of what drove me to nail things down for the sake of security is our lack of leadership, which I think is getting worse, not better. I'm especially leery of where the leadership is taking us financially. I don't think they really care whether or not we are secure in our own finances, or our retirement years.

Yet, while I feel very uneasy about where things are going, I feel very certain that the only place where your retirement would be safe is with David Reindel's kind of program.

But I've also heard that you can get into the wrong kind of annuity, so you need a real expert. Yes, a stock broker would like to sell you an annuity, too. But this is Dave's passion. Annuities are all he does. I've since learned that he knows more about annuities than anybody does, so this man gives me confidence, which is something I haven't had in years. I'm suddenly at ease because, through David, I know where I'm going to be in five years, and when you know where you're going, you can begin to adjust to the kind of lifestyle you'll be able to depend on. That, to me, is worth more than being in a casino spinning a roulette wheel. That's a fact, that's a given, that's elementary.

Just look at Reindel's approach and you will see the logic: It's a controlled environment that is going to go one way, and to me there could be no more secure way than that. For me, the days of playing roulette in the stock market are pretty much limited. I still have some money in the market but not a lot, maybe $35,000, which I can put into play and afford to lose. I feel comfortable with that, and I still have a small annuity account with the last brokerage worth about $20,000—because when I was with them, I made some gains.

The stocks I have are through a company called the Money Paper, a company that will buy you your first stock with the right purchase plan. The company helps you purchase that first share with a very minimal fee, so once you get the statement back with that first share, you can invest in that company.

Some of these companies (through Money Paper) have no fee. Trading in General Electric stock, for example, the fee is $3 no matter how much you invest, whether it's $10 or $10,000. Another part of my stock portfolio is in Exxon-Mobile and there's no fee at all; you put money in and they invest in the market every week, any amount of money for zero fees—although coming back out when you sell costs five cents per share. And these aren't small-time stocks, either. You buy directly from Exxon-Mobile without having to go through a mutual fund and from there I've gone into Coca-Cola, Pfizer and General Electric.

I bring this up because I think, after the last crash, people are really fed up with the hype and ridiculous fees of traditional brokers. Since the crash, this is the way a lot of us are going to trade, if we still trade at all after a certain age, and on that note, I do think more and more people are going into annuities. I think a lot of annuity carriers are going to get a lot more competitive and innovative to meet the demand.

I have one, last thing to say about David versus the other brokerage entity I was with. When I first spoke to my last broker about moving money out of there, they wanted to know where I was going. They sternly warned me about "playing around with my money" and said I needed to keep my money in shares of stock, so that I would have some money to leave my daughter.

They kept pressing me to tell them what I was going to do until I finally said I was going into annuities. You should have seen the change in atmosphere. They said "Annuities?! What?! Are you sure that's what you want to do?" They talked about the so-called "high fees" and said I was making a mistake.

This is the kind of thing you might have to face if you decide to get out of the casino. I stood my ground and said it was no mistake. I said I'd been talking to David Reindel, who had explained things to me like no one ever had. I said I'd spoken to other people about annuities before and that this guy "really knows his stuff."

They said I was being sold a bill of goods and I said, "I don't think so." I'm saying this because some people might have to hang tough when getting out of the market. On that note, you're about to find out how nasty things can get.

My stock broker at the time asked me for a chance to stay with her. She said she would talk to her supervisor—her head of sales—about what I was going to do. She said she had some annuities she could sell me but needed to talk to someone about it—because she probably didn't know much about annuities in the first place. But still I gave her a chance.

What happened next still lingers in my memory. After getting hold of her supervisor, she and called me back and said that when she brought up the mere word "annuities," he threw up his arms, turned around and—over his shoulder—said, "Who understands annuities? Then she said he just walked out of the room. He didn't even want to talk about it. This was the supervisor of my last and final brokerage firm.

After that, she changed altogether, saying, "If it sounds like it's too good to be true, it probably is." They were so desperate to keep me there. I don't like to lose accounts, either, but she had nothing to counter David's common sense, nothing more to offer, no ammunition. Instead, they do what they always do. They go back to the so-called high fees with annuities. High fees? What about monthly broker fees? How about endless, nickel and dime fees associated with mutual funds? What about the so-called gains you get after suffering horrendous losses, which will happen again and again.

With the annuities I have with Dave, I get 7 percent when the market is up. I lose nothing when the market is down. They add bonuses to offset things like the 5% fee when you're ready to come out of the annuity and take distributions. What you get in contributions from the company, in addition to 7 percent gains when they happen, is well above the 5 percent as you draw money out.

As we speak, the Dow is above 12,000 again and above 13,000 now and then, but we're still being threatened by—what is it this time? —more trouble in foreign economies? Gee, I forget. Who wants to remember? I don't have to anymore.

Back to my stock broker, I always liked her. She had always seemed very professional and I thought we had a friendship, but when I approached her with this annuity strategy, she finally turned into someone who seemed to be in cahoots with the devil. The difference was day and night and I could hardly believe it was the same person: She was awfully nasty in the end, which goes to show that these people are not only poorly informed, they really are not looking out for your best interest.

I now know first-hand that they may come across as being knowledgeable, but they're really not. And in the end, the broker was blinded by the potential of losing the account. That's really all she could see, and I'm still disappointed by the way she conducted herself—after doing a complete 180 turnaround from being the nicest person you would ever want to meet, to a person you would not want to have in your life. I could not believe it.

But that's all behind me now. My 42-year-old daughter works in a hospital and has three children in their teens and early 20s. What's most important to me now is that I will not become a burden to them because my income will not play out before I pass away. And I will have something to pass along to them, other than bitter stories about the money I lost in the market.

I still remember a quote by Ronald Reagan when he predicted what might happen to the future of our economy and American retirees. Reagan said something about, "freedom being very fragile and that we could be one generation away from losing it." It seemed like a cryptic remark at the time, but it remains one that rings hauntingly true today. He made a number of statements like that, indicating that he'd heard "whispers in the corridors" about what was in the wind.

I think we see now what had been in the works long ago. Now we need to prepare.

#

Taking a Side Road with Another Solution

This is a timely moment to add the following interview from my weekly "Don't Die Broke" radio show.

Because so many people lost so much during the Crash of 2008, they need to be reminded that options are always out there, one being the fallback income available through our own home equity.

I realize that many people have tragically lost their homes to foreclosure, yet I'm hoping that a good number of those foreclosures involved younger homeowners, people who took advantage of a liberal era in mortgage lending. I say I "hope" most of them were younger because even in our mid-40s, there would be enough earning years ahead to recover, albeit in a more modest home, which was part of the problem to begin with, right? Too many people were persuaded to get into homes they really couldn't afford in the long-run.

For many people in or near retirement, we're really looking at a different equation. Many people in this situation might have lost heavily in the 2008 crash, but they still have a great deal of equity in their home. They might even have their home mortgage paid down to nothing, or nearly nothing.

In that case, or in situations where market losses have left people with more modest retirements than they had originally hoped for, the following advice might very well apply to them.

At least the newer version of the much discussed "reverse mortgage" is something to consider. The reverse mortgage was full of holes in years past, in my opinion. Yet, much has been done to correct this product, with a great many consumer protections now built in that were not there in the past.

As always, be sure to shop. You might also consider having an attorney look over any reverse mortgage agreement before you sign it. After all, it's still a mortgage, and it still involves what may be the last remaining, major asset for many, after the crash.

That having been said, I can't think of anyone more knowledgeable about the reverse mortgage than our next guest, Jerry Delmato, a 33-year veteran of the banking industry and a reverse mortgage specialist since 2004.

To all survivors: Hang in there and please consider what Jerry has to say!

David Reindel

Jerry Delmato:

I'll be brief. A reverse mortgage is an economic option that can enhance the quality of life for homeowners over age 62.

It's a federally insured loan that provides access to some of the equity in a person's home, and here's the key: It requires no repayment as long as the borrowers live in the house, pay the taxes, pay the homeowner's insurance, and keep the home in good repair. As long as those things are done, no repayment is required.

There are misconceptions about the reverse mortgage of today. Sometimes people regurgitate information from long ago. Yet, while reverse mortgages are a wonderful opportunity for some people, they are not for everybody. To really get the facts, you need to talk to a specialist, not a part-timer, not somebody who's done it for maybe three months, but somebody with experience.

The biggest myth about a reverse mortgage is that if you get into this kind of loan, you are giving the house to the bank. In fact, the myth that the bank owns the home is totally incorrect. Like any other mortgage, the borrower retains title to the home. The bank merely has a lien against the house and anytime the borrower wants to pay off the lien, they can. They just pay off the loan and the house is theirs.

When I first got into the reverse mortgage business, my employer said it was a life-changing benefit. Maybe that's a bit of an exaggeration, but over the years I've been able to see that it can be a life-changing product in the right kind of situation. Simply keep in mind that from the day after closing, NO HOUSE PAYMENTS WILL BE REQUIRED, as long as the borrower lives in the house. The reverse mortgage of today also has a lot of flexibility. Just because you make one choice at the beginning doesn't mean you can't change it.

Still, there are three basic ways that you can access funds: a lump sum, you can take out all the money that's available to you on Day One, or you can take a large chunk on Day One. The second option creates a line of credit; you have money pre-approved in your name and you can access it in the amounts and time frames that you desire. The third option is that you would receive a monthly check or direct deposit to your bank account, which would be made on the first day of every month.

My clients use reverse mortgages in many different ways. The primary purpose is the common denominator of getting financial piece of mind to supplement their income, or to pay off their mortgage and eliminate the payment that goes along with it. Others use it to pay off credit card balances.

Details are many, of course, but that's essentially how it works. Again, the reverse mortgage is not for everyone and a reverse mortgage specialist will tell you just that. But if you find yourself in need of supplementing your situation in retirement, it might work for you.

Again, never be afraid to ask about someone's experience and credentials if they represent themselves as a reverse mortgage specialist.

(Editor's note: Some of the comments above include excerpts from our "Don't Die Broke" radio show, which include aired segments that may be found on our web site: www.davidreindel.com.

#

CHAPTER 7

The New Financial Normal

By Dave Reindel

Before moving on to our next "reality in retirement" subject, let me go over a few things that have become almost a given. As many of us know all too well, the Great Recession of 2008 essentially changed the ground rules for retirement.

Because so many dearly held financial strategies plainly failed, we now recognize the post-2008 recession era as being something of a paradigm shift in itself. Yet, some of us still cling to idea that, even in a this global economy, another economic collapse might somehow bypass the United States. Or, we might think that economic troubles in foreign countries will have no effect on American markets and retirement assets.

The same people see the crash of 2008 as an exception to the rule, thinking that another economic cataclysm is not likely to occur again in our lifetime. Fact is, no nation is insulated from the fragile economics of the next market swing, and this is a new thing. Taking this fundamental into account, the world is less secure in a financial sense than ever before. Global political events clearly affect Wall Street every day. Libya enters revolutionary turmoil and political upheaval, causing oil prices to rise, which, in turn, spurs analysts to worry about oil becoming the potential trigger of a new recession.

Too many of us have already forgotten about what happened before it all went down in 2008: There were numerous, smaller small cash-quakes all over global markets, before the big one hit us in that unsettling autumn of a bygone age of retirement investment.

If you are 50, 60, or 70, how are you saving for retirement? Are you doing the same things over and over again, hoping things will get better when they really won't? Are you trying to save but really not getting anywhere?

If you are reading this, you might be in that boat because part of what's going on is happening in the stock market. It's a different market today. Aside the potential for global-financial catastrophe, markets today are not really designed for individual investors. The hedge funds, the rapid traders, these are the guys who are controlling what's going on. If I trade I might win if I'm lucky, but I probably won't.

Some of us are moving into bonds and bond-like annuities, which is sort of what we do. So, there are solutions besides the stock market. There are guaranteed income solutions.

As a result, we work every day with my clients, people who do not worry one day about what's going on with the stock market because they know what will happen: Their principal is protected, which is a big deal. I would much rather have a percentage of a gain and no loss, as opposed to having a gains-loss-gains-loss-gains-loss, and wind up with plus-two percent instead minus 20 percent.

Some mutual fund companies are trying to respond to what's going on with Absolute Return Funds, Volatile Index Funds and other programs. Absolute Return Funds, according to the *Wall Street Journal*, are not always what they appear to be. They're diversified, very complex portfolios designed to split the difference between stock and bond market risk, and they call them Absolute Return Funds. They deliver mid-single-digit returns of, say, 5 percent, given stock market volatility, and the goal is to reduce risk to the point that they return 1 percent over Treasuries.

One percent over treasuries right now is only 3.9 percent. Big deal. Their holdings are emerging markets, bonds, treasuries, municipals, hedge funds, private equity, real estate investment trusts, currency and debt of emerging markets, and interest only mortgage derivatives. Does this sound scary to you? It does to me.

Of the 21 funds offering Absolute Return Funds, the gains averaged .017 percent for the first six months of 2010. I just don't think this makes a lot of sense. I think the risk-reward ratio is too great.

So let's talk about annuities and debunk some of the still lingering, disinformation out there.

We use specific annuities for income. We also use highly rated companies. We want to make sure these guys are going to be around for a long time. One, in fact, has been around since 1696, but they're all legal reserve companies, so they have assets in reserve to back up what they say, because they're insurance companies. This is how insurance companies operate.

Yet even now, even as million and millions of Americans flock to annuities, I'm hard pressed to find any newspaper, including the *Wall Street Journal*, where the word annuity is routinely mentioned and I don't understand it. In this environment and especially in relation to the rest, the annuity is the path to security and it's the path to predictability and certainty.

I think media and securities investment advocates still share a traditional bias against insurance in general. Whether it be property casualty insurance, or any kind of insurance, I see bias based on the notion that insurance companies are making out better than the consumer so they must not be a good bet for the consumer.

I would like to pose some basic logic to that argument. First, the insurance industry is a highly regulated industry, regulated by 50 states individually. When a new insurance company comes into your state with a product to present, the state looks very carefully at the product and the company to be sure that the product treats the consumer fairly and—this is often overlooked by media—it makes sure the insurance company *can afford* to offer it.

Okay, a lot of this comes from misunderstanding and the hard work of people in opposing camps, people who lead ingenious and effective campaigns of anti-insurance disinformation. Yet, if you read about mutual funds, sometimes the facts aren't so accurate because mutual funds don't have to be as factual as we would like them to be.

As far as information management involving securities and insurance products, I think you'll see a lot of changes because of what's going on in the economy.

Consumers must be able to better differentiate between income annuities, immediate annuities, fixed indexed annuities and variable annuities. There are all kinds out there and they offer a swarm of different features. As many in this industry know, my favorite are fixed index annuities because we have some of the upside gain and protection of principal, and my clients have been very happy with this type of product. Yet, there are various formulas available with these, as with any annuity, but all we seem to read about are caps and fees supposedly leveraged against the consumer.

In truth, caps and fees are simply based on what companies can afford to buy in the option market. That is what predicts the formula. If you look at formulas for all the different insurance companies, they will look very similar because the companies are all doing basically the same thing. They can't take advantage of the consumer based on rumor-based, arbitrary information, like some in other financial sectors, meaning you won't hear about "hot tips" related to annuities because product formulas are designed around what carriers can pay for options, which depends on market volatility. But annuities don't penalize consumers for volatility by reducing accumulated principal. When the market goes down, annuity earnings flat-line during the down cycle. That's it. They come back when the market begins to rise.

Is this better than a minus-10 percent, or greater, reverse of principal? Of course it is. If I have $100,000, I might have zero gain for a time, but if the market is down 20 percent, I'm not going to lose $20,000, either. And I still get my guarantee, whether it's 2 percent or 6 percent.

No, you won't make that 20% gain when the market soars, but you won't lose 20 percent when the market plummets, either. We build with guarantees against loss to ensure future income. That's what you come to me for. You need a secure place for your money, which wasn't working for people with CDs at 1 percent, was it?

So, with CDs, we have one extreme at 1% percent earnings, then we have market highs on the other side. But with the market, you have no way of knowing what to expect, especially given the future prognosis of an increasingly integrated global economy.

Annuities are squarely in the middle. Right now, when things go well, annuities work like this: I had clients in March, 2010, that had made 18 percent to 21 percent in gains. The reason they did so well was due to the fact that the market was so bad in 2008. So they got that gain, and the gains were locked in; they cannot be erased, but that's not going to happen every year with index annuities.

My clients know that. I tell them that. It will average out over the years. These products are designed to give you a fair rate of return in the 5 percentile range, the 6 percentile range, in that realm. They're not designed to give those pie-in-the-sky returns we've all heard about.

In terms of the indexing, using the S&P option, there's no downside, only upside—or, "flat-side" when the market tanks (but no loss). That's hard for people to get their arms around. I had some clients come in to see me yesterday and they said, are we going to lose money on our annuity? They still didn't get it. Because their friends have all lost money in the stock market, they can't understand why they can't lose money with their annuities. They are in their second year with me and I tell them, "No," every time they ask about the potential for market loss. So, it takes a while for things to sink in, but I am always very careful when I sit down and talk about a potential client's situation.

Before recommending anything to you, I make sure YOU understand what I'm talking about. In that vein, in order to help clarify what I've been saying about fragile financial environments and global economies, I asked my friend Fran Tarkenton to weigh in on the subject during a recent interview on my radio show, *Don't Die Broke*.

#

FRAN TARKENTON & "THE GREEK TRAGEDY"

By Fran Tarkenton

(with Dave Reindel on "Don't Die Broke")

I want to pick up where Dave left off about the need for annuities in the coming global economy. We're in it for good and we're in for a whole new set of ground rules for retirement.

If you call what's happening to socialist Europe a come-uppance, Greece is the first casualty, where you have one in four people in Greece who are government employees.

You cannot sustain a society by having one out of four people working for the government. You take 25 percent of the people out of the work force and it's not sustainable. In Spain, it's one out of five, and Spain is going to default all of its notes, right after Greece.

What's happening is that the welfare state of Europe, the socialist agenda of Europe, is a wonderful thing, right? Nobody is going to have to work!

They can have a four-day work week, six-hour work days, sing Kumbaya and have a wonderful non-productive life, which has been happening throughout Europe.

Only now you can see the results in Greece and Spain and, although it's not like it's going you happen to America, we have to learn from history. We have to learn from what's happening in other parts of the world, because the world has closed in.

We cannot let this happen to our country. Are we going to make housing available for everyone whether you can afford or not? No, because we cannot take care of the whole world. We can NOT spread the tax base to accommodate more people, and I think we're getting that message out. I hope we are.

Reindel: We have to look in the mirror, Fran. We have budget problems here. New Jersey's budget deficit is $750 million and while they're trying to cut back and they're getting resistance, you can't spend money you don't have. At the end of the day, you pay your bills, you pay yourself, and there should be some profit.

Dave is right. The government produces nothing. It's a drag on everybody else. I was out in California several weeks ago on Laguna Beach and realized that I was in a state of 30 million people, about 13 percent of the US population. It has great brain power in Silicon Valley, the technology capital of the world, the envy of the world. You have the San Joaquin Valley which has the most fertile soil in the world. This is a state with the greatest natural resources, great human resources, and yet the State of California is bankrupt because they tried to provide services for everybody. For example, a free college education for everybody is a wonderful thing to offer, but we can't do that. It's not sustainable.

And now our other states are saying that they have to cut services, and that they have to cut back on expenses. Luckily, some have been able to do it, but people need to realize that we're in a HUGE transition, both at the state level and the federal level, because not only do we have to stop increasing spending, we have to cut it back. We have to make our voices heard. We cannot be the silent majority anymore. We've got to put people—Democrat or Republican or Independent—back into Washington, back into our state houses, who are going to listen to us and stop the insanity and stop the spending, and I really believe this is happening all across the country.

Reindel: We're in some perilous times right now. People I talk to in their 50s and 60s want to retire and be comfortable, but there are so many political risks today. People are worried and they're nervous. What, today, will affect my retirement the most?

Interesting, if you find yourself reading this book after Obama leaves the White House, what changes will have occurred? Any changes? If some have happened, government has very likely come up with other ways to risk our future in retirement. I believe that for all people retired today, the one thing you have to have is a plan to insure that you don't run out of money. All of us want to put off that kind of planning because we're afraid of any kind of risk, but there are risks in all generations of life, and people have to be ready for some kind of risk.

I also think that America and the people of America will always find ways to move forward, but the reality today (*during the Obama administration when this book was written*) is that we have an administration in Washington but we don't know who they are. We don't know much about their background. We do know that we've been seeing a political atmosphere that is not pro-business, not a government that understands business, not a leadership that really seems to understand free-market capitalism. This is an administration that is moving us closer to government control of our lives, and all we have to do is look at Europe to see where it will lead.

The history of civilization shows that the more government control you have, the worse things tend to get. It has been said that if you put the government in charge of the Sahara Desert, they would find a way to run out of sand. I think there's a great risk for all of us today as we see the government raise taxes, take over health care, add 1,600 IRS agents to help monitor health care—and pay for it all by sucking money out of things like the Social Security surplus, which has been going on for a long time.

Can we count on the government to insure us against going broke in retirement? No way. Just look at Greece and Spain, and the way we're now tied into their economies and the way they do business.

The only way to insure against going *broke before you die* is to insure your own money against the next economic collapse, both in this country and around the world.

(Editor's note: Some of the comments above include excerpts from our "Don't Die Broke" radio show, which include aired segments that may be found on our web site: www.davidreindel.com)

#

CHAPTER 8

How to Be Happy in Retirement

After the dire observations Fran Tarkenton and I made in the past chapter, let's settle down and hear from someone who has it all in perspective.

The following individual knows exactly what I'm talking about when it comes to annuities, financial safety and security. Her name is Anne, and at age 76, Anne has been through many variations on investment markets, the perils of running a business and risk in general.

This widowed, former retirement home director has seen what can happen when retirees fail to plan for security. She has seen what happens when people run out of money before they die.

This profile is accordingly more about the sensation of freedom and reward one can have with the right kind of plan. Anne offers more than a few solid lessons along the way and this is her story.

May Yours Be As Successful,

David Reindel

*   *   *

Anne:

I like to reflect on life's lessons from time to time and one of things I frequently note is the way so many people say they wish they'd done certain things when they were younger.

I didn't make that mistake. Every year I'd take a trip, sometimes to Europe, sometimes around this country of ours. I've always tried to do what's important to me. I don't want to leave this planet with regrets because I didn't do things I wanted to do.

I went to New Zealand and Australia, to the Great Barrier Reef and the Sydney Opera House. I've enjoyed lots of partying, saw the penguins near Melbourne, then went back to the southern island of New Zealand, which probably has the prettiest scenery I've ever been in.

I've been to England a number of times because my background is there, and I wound up writing to some English pen pals, one in particular who has been over here to see me; and I've been over there to travel around Scotland with them, which was very exciting.

What would eventually lead me to Dave Reindel began in 1994. I had invested some money in a rather conservative bank and it wasn't doing very well. After that, I actually met Dave at a seminar—in those days he made house calls—and he met with my second husband who was 13 years my senior and up there in years. He was a retired Navy man who had some investments in a company in California, which weren't doing well financially. In fact, the company was in trouble so Dave moved some money out of there for us, and that was the beginning of our relationship.

Through Dave, we first made a move into an F&G annuity—we were with F&G until about five years ago—when we went with a 10-year fixed annuity offered by Allianz. I almost always go with Dave's recommendations, but that kind of trust doesn't come easily. Number one, you have to have trust in someone and I've learned to trust that Dave's stays up on things.

When he suggested moving money from F&G into Allianz, he'd done a lot of research. I knew we'd be starting all over again but it was important to me to go with a company that could do the best for me, and with the new annuity, if I needed to start taking income at age 80, this particular 10-year annuity would let me do that. Mainly, I want to enjoy my life and, to me, happiness is all about knowing what will be happening in the future.

I've read the annuity statements once a year and during last two years—during the recession—the statements have been pretty flat, but I know a number of people who have lost a lot of money over the same two-year period. I haven't. Need I say more? So, I have to be satisfied with that, although there were moments before that when I knew of people making good amounts of money before the crash.

But, again, after the crash I had such a great relief in knowing my money was safe. I've made enough from my investments to take trips and have a good life. I really have. Of course, it helps that my husband was a retired Navy man. He retired after 30 years with a Navy pension and died at 87 over a year ago. So, I have another income plus a very tiny retirement of my own, plus Social security. All in all, I've been able to live rather comfortably and haven't had to touch that (annuity) money at all. I probably won't have to touch that money unless something catastrophic happens, and that's what it's for.

Given my husband's age, we did have a long term care insurance policy that Dave suggested we have. I thought it was a good idea because my husband was so much older than I. Then my husband had a stroke and was dead three days later so we never had to use it, but I maintain it today.

(Audrey is well set with the LTC policy since it began years ago. It will prevent her from paying down all other assets if going to a nursing home, and if the cost of premium becomes a problem, Audrey will have the yet untouched annuity to fall back on).

Today I just paint. I love to paint. I paints the walls in my house and I love painting fine art pictures. I've been painting walls today because I've decided to re-do my kitchen. As for fine art, my painting style is very contemporary. I like to work with color and some rather realistic art as well.

The point is that I AM retired and I have the time. I could only dabble with art before retirement. Now I very much enjoy it and have a studio downstairs in the basement with good light. Now that I live alone, I just go downstairs and paint to my heart's content and just lose myself in it. So, there's a good hint for people in retirement: Anybody who has any creativity is so fortunate, I have always said. I can always find something to do even though I live alone, and because of that, I'm not a lonely person. My art has even led me to have people try to coax me into showing some of my work.

As for my finances, I leave them to my attorney and I feel comfortable with Dave. I have to have someone. I know how to save money but really not how to invest it comfortably, so I trust Dave to invest it for me, and although it's not making a great deal of money it hasn't lost anything. That has become so important, more important than making money because I have what I need to enjoy life. At the same time, many of my contemporaries had money in their 401 k s and have lost so much of it. Now, they're envious.

The lesson, here, is that the most important thing is to do what makes you happy, of course, but living beyond one's means is not a good idea and I have always been on the conservative side as far as always putting some money away. Again, I don't have a lot of money but I have a comfortable amount, and I try to instill in my children to always have a little put aside for a rainy day. I also advise to NOT put all your money into real estate or anything else, and, when you're my age, to preserve what you have in something safe.

Besides that, to have hobbies and lots of friends in retirement is important, maybe more important than having a lot of money, so that on the day you do retire you will have some things—some favorite activities—to fall back on. There are so many kinds of activities that don't necessarily cost a lot of money.

These days, I don't even try to budget. I just know how much my income is per month and if I spend all of it that's fine because I don't touch my savings, and things have worked out well so far. I did do some work on the house this year. I built a garage and I'm renovating the kitchen, using money from a CD that wasn't making any money. It was time to replace the old garage, which was down the hill behind the house, because we couldn't get up the hill in winter. So, now it's a workshop and the new garage is finally level with the street.

To be honest, I wouldn't have done it when my husband was alive because he was a super tight budgeter and I didn't want to upset him. But because of my other income and savings, I felt that I could do this. The renovation is part of what I consider a necessary plan. I've not only added value to the house with the two-car garage, a renovated kitchen would be a must if I ever need to sell the house. I had already done the bathroom, very conservatively, but the kitchen is not so conservative—we're doing a bang-up job in the kitchen. And it has all been possible through conservative planning. Those have been my major projects and the rest is secure.

To feel really secure, you have to find someone you can really work with. If I have questions, Dave is always there, and knowledgeable and never pushy. He's trustworthy, his wife works with him and I've found both of them to be very, very good people to work with through the years.

I say this after working with other people. When I call Dave and his wife, they either pick up the telephone or get right back to me, and when statements come in, Dave is on the phone with me, answering any questions I might have, explaining what it's all about. But the main thing is trust, which also means you have to feel that someone has the best interest of his clients at heart, and that's Dave.

I've heard people say that, "Well, these (financial planners) all make money; they don't do it for free." I understand that, but some people don't. I've had friends who don't want to go with an advisor because they're making money, but that's ridiculous. We all have to make money. The reason I went with Dave is that I've been through advisors with different levels of knowledge, and I felt that when we first met Dave he just knew his stuff. We talked about the fact that we needed to get the money out of the losing company in California and he *clearly* explained to us how our annuities would work. We understood everything he said, and we just felt that it was the safer thing to do.

But with annuities, you have to be careful, too. There are all kinds of annuities, so you really need an expert in the annuity field. The same thing goes for any other kind of financial product, of course.

The way I feel now, going flat with an annuity is better than losing money. I didn't have much money of my own when I met my second husband because my first husband bankrupted us with a fly-by-night business. When I divorced him, I didn't have a dime to my name, which is why I went to work for the senior center. I've learned about saving money the hard way, you might say.

One day I marched into a bank and asked what would be the least amount of money I could borrow. The banker asked what I would use it for and I said I wanted to buy some antiques. He said I could borrow $500, so I borrowed $500. But I really did it so I could establish credit and get a credit card.

That was in 1979, and from that point on, I immediately started putting money into a savings account. I put away as much money as I could and although I didn't make much money back then, at the retirement home, I did pretty well.

While I did that I also had another job that allowed us to go on an occasional trip. We had to save like crazy—to be able to go to Europe, for example—but you have to sacrifice when you're younger, in order to do things like that.

That kind of sacrifice also lets you save for retirement, and all I can say is that it is certainly is a relief when you get older not to have to worry about where your next meal is coming from, whether you'll be able to afford your medication, whether it's going to be medication or food this week, which a lot of people have to worry about.

I've always tried to do everything I could and do it right, which, again, is why I went with Dave. You have to have the right people on your side. You just do.

Other than that, it's hard to tell everybody how to be happy. We all have to find happiness in our own way. Unfortunately, too many people just don't know how, no matter how much money they have. On the other hand, without going overboard financially you need money because if you don't have any, you can't be happy. So, it's a balancing act. It was easier to save a few years ago as opposed to now.

As for saving money today, I have three children and they're all struggling because the economy is just awful and everything costs so much money. My children are 55, 53 and 46. My 46-year-old daughter was in Hawaii in the real estate business when it went belly-up and now she's trying to live in Hawaii with no job, which is really awful. My oldest daughter lives in Salem, Oregon, works for a local art association and while she has never made a lot of money, she's very happy because she does what she likes to do. Now, my middle child is 53 and was laid off from his job with NASA as an engineering fabricator. Right now, he grabs whatever is available to supplement his meager unemployment check.

What do you tell adult children in this recession? It's a tough economy and all I can say to them is to hang in there, but sometimes I have to help them out. He's going through a divorce so he's staying with me for a while, but I tell my son that times will get better and I know this because we've been through two world wars in this country, and the Great depression. We can get through this.

Yet, history repeats itself and while we don't want a recession to ever happen again, the younger generations will not have gone through this. I'm afraid they'll forget what we're going through now and things will start all over again. History will repeat itself, unfortunately.

(Reindel: Well put, Anne. Every 15 years or so, economies fail and that's why we put people like Anne into annuities. While she has more than enough to fall back on from other sources, her annuity just might be able to help her children in the future. It's also important to remember the post-9/11 crash, the 1987 crash, the mini-crash in 1998, the 1999 S&P crash, and all of the mini corrections leading up to 2007, when people everywhere were in such denial about the economic bubble we'd enjoyed for so long. Meanwhile, there will always be "experts" distracting us away from savings-oriented financial advisors. On that, we'll give Anne the final word.)

I have a friend who works for Merrill Lynch and believe me, there were times when I thought it would be good to have him invest my money. But I'm glad I never did because they were in trouble too, as we all know.

It's much better to be conservative with your money instead of trying to make a lot of money all at once. Maybe that works for some people but I know it doesn't work with me and now I'm glad. I know I have to be conservative in order to have any money, and be happy because of it, because I'm not that knowledgeable about it. I have to trust somebody trustworthy and Dave Reindel has been that person for me.

#

Another "Long Term" Alternative

Because Anne and her husband were an appropriate fit for long term care insurance—given their difference in ages—I thought it appropriate to answer some questions people might have about this type of insurance.

Keep in mind that not everyone may be right for a long term care policy. Some may wait too long for a policy to be affordable. Also, some insurance policies, and some annuity policies, might contain special provisions to handle nursing home costs, as well as in-home, long-term care costs.

Annuities have also proven useful in protecting assets from spend-down requirements per state Medicaid programs. So there is much to consider and every situation is different.

My following guest is very knowledgeable about this type of policy and offers a few basics you might want to consider before delving into the subject.

His name is Sean McFadden and he is with Lincoln Financial Distributors, a company providing long term care insurance to appropriate individuals along the eastern seaboard and nationwide.

As always, take your time gathering the facts, and be prepared to ask lots of questions.

David Reindel

Sean McFadden:

The probabilities of needing long term care are high. The Department of Health and Human Services did a survey in 2007, which found that 70 percent of Americans aged 65 and older are going to need some kind of long term care in their lifetime. Imagine sitting at a dinner party with 10 of your friends and realizing that seven out of 10, including yourself, are going to need long-term care. It's big number, a shocking number.

Costs are high. Long term care insurance can be the single biggest ticket on a retirement portfolio. You have to prepare for it because the following nursing home costs are only national averages from a 2007 survey, and could have risen considerably by now: In 2007, average nursing home costs ran $66,000 a year for a shared room. A private room cost an average of $75,000. However, a lot of people think that long-term care means staying in a nursing home. This is sometimes the case, yet, long term care can begin in your home, and in-home care can last for a long period of time.

There are a lot of great products out there that provide for care in your home—maybe somebody coming in to take care of the groceries, or help with bathing. The cost of having somebody come in and help at home is about $25 an hour and these costs can add up, but they may be preferable to nursing home care.

Again, the probability and cost of long term care are both high.

Reindel: For couples, an important feature is in-home health care, because nobody wants a loved one to go into a nursing home. That's what people are going to try to use first. Beyond that, here's the real world: For a client going into assisted living the cost is around $4,000 a month, not inexpensive at all. If you plan for this, it's going to be okay, so it's important to act, not react, and have a plan in place. Yet, what are the options?

There are various options for people out there today. The first option is to do nothing. Doing nothing is being reactive. Call it self-insurance; if something happens, you are going to pay for it out of your own portfolio and that's a risk.

Another option is insurance for traditional long term care. There are some great products out there. Once a person qualifies, meaning that if you cannot perform the six activities of daily living, or if you have severe cognitive impairment like Alzheimer's, you will be reimbursed for long term care services.

You pay a monthly premium for long term care insurance, and the downside is that if you never need LTC, you get no benefit, unless you include a return-of-premium rider. In that case, you can get some money back.

Recent new products include what we call "link of benefit" features. These products link the benefits of long term care policies and life insurance, offer to pay costs and act like life insurance, accruing value if you don't need long term care.

Just something to think about as you put together the insurance-related part of your portfolio.

(Editor's note: The comments above include excerpts from our "Don't Die Broke" radio show, which include aired segments that may be found on our web site: www.davidreindel.com)

\#

CHAPTER 9

The Decision That Saved a Retirement

My friend and client Robert did what everybody did before the Crash of 2008, which could have cost him his retirement.

Then he did the ONE right thing that meant EVERYTHING in the end.

Robert is 74 and retired after working for a major office supply company for most of his life. Now living the good life in Rhode Island, he is widowed and has two children aged 54 and 53.

Thanks to making the right move, he will be able to live the life he wants to live and leave something to his children. Therefore, I consider Robert's plan one kind of model you may want to consider if your situation is similar to his.

As you can see after reading this far, each retirement model is different, but one or two elements remain the same. Annuities achieve some of the best results available for either asset preservation, or guaranteed income, or both.

For Your Future,

David Reindel

*   *   *

Robert:

I've been working with Dave for at least 10 years and I have an annuity with Dave. As with probably most of his clients, I met Dave through a seminar he put on. This one happened to be in Providence, Rhode Island, near my home.

I had been searching for a vehicle for my retirement, so he came over to the house after the seminar, with his wife Janet, and began to explain his strategy with annuities. Dave really takes time to explain everything with real clarity. He doesn't rush through anything, nor does he cause anyone to rush to judgment.

It took him three or four visits before I was convinced that this is what I should have done with some of my money at that particular time. So I invested with him and, with that particular annuity, even today, it offers different areas where you can put your money.

This one also has an earnings guarantee of 3 percent every year, which I like because it will help keep up with inflation. That's a base earnings guarantee, and, of course, you have your guaranteed safety of principal, which made all the difference during the recession.

I was fortunate. I made a decision before we had this latest recession crisis. I was determined to go the safe way with an annuity. I also locked into the minimum 3 percent annual earnings, rather than choose a lesser guarantee in favor of a higher earnings cap, which can be great when the market is up but can go flat when it's down—you never lose anything, of course, but I'd rather be locked into some kind of guaranteed gain.

Mainly, and I can't say this enough, I did not lose any of the principal I put into the annuity in the last recession. Nor did I lose any principal or accumulated earnings over several smaller recessions and market drops during the past decade, include the Great Recession of 2008.

All this time, after we had all this set up, Dave has been on the phone with me every year, through the years, and he helped me tremendously in that section of my portfolio. Today, I have roughly 40 percent of my retirement assets in Dave Reindel's annuity, an Aviva VisionMark Advantage Annuity, and I've already started taking income.

At the same time I went with David, which was several years ago, I had other money invested in municipal bonds, but I don't have any money in the stock market today. I haven't had money in the stock market for years. I don't like to take risk. The bonds and annuities have all done very well.

I like the municipal bonds I chose because they will go up and if you keep them until the maturity date, you get your principal back. They've maintained their distribution rate right along. I'm getting, on average, right around 5% percent. Again, I have quite a few municipal bonds around the country and they've performed very well. No problem at all.

So I do diversify away from annuities, while leveraging the guarantees annuities can offer. I think they're an important part of any retirement package. But you have to look carefully at each one. This is no place to consult with someone inexperienced.

David knows the annuities that he's involved with. He shared with us the difference in annuities. He gave us the information and let us come up with our own decisions, and when I've had questions, he has always been there, right by the phone. Anytime I call about anything to do with the annuity, he calls right back with answers, which, from what I hear from other people with other planners, is sort of unusual. In that way, David has been like a friend, I would say.

Over the years I've been in stocks of all kinds. It's my personal opinion—after starting years ago with stocks—that most of the people I've dealt with in financial services are in business to make money, with not always the client's best interest at heart. They're all in it to make money, but some are more helpful than others, so I more or less did it myself and planned as I went along for many years.

In municipal bonds, I had a friend who happened to be working with state and municipal governments and is not a financial services advisor. He was the one who got me interested in municipal bonds and I gradually went into that area, so that's where the larger part of my portfolio is now. I'm very happy with that. I don't plan on changing at all. I'm doing my retirement planning with just what I have here now because I know what kind of income I have coming in, and I don't care to risk any of it in the stock market. Meaning, I'm set with what I have, and I'm happy to say that I know I'm going to keep what I have.

When looking for any kind of financial advisor, or any type of related investment, for that matter, I think it depends greatly on the age of the individual who is looking for the advisor and investment. Depending on their age, it might be a good idea to get into stocks if they're in their 30s or 40s. The market, as we all know, is on the upturn right now and I think this will continue for a while. As we all know, this works if you can put up with the swings in the markets, and if you can sleep at night taking the losses and gains.

However, I think that regardless of what kind of vehicle they go into, and regardless of age, people who want to invest need to do their own homework. I know that a lot of people are busy with families, and some husbands and wives hold two jobs, but it behooves one of them to know what's going on and not to rely 100 percent on a financial advisor. You can pick one and let them know what your goals are, and I believe strongly that families need to get involved—and not just go by the Dow Jones average.

As we know, the Dow is up quite high again, but that's only representative of about 30 stocks. So we hear it all the time—that the market is up and that some of the stocks that were low last year have doubled. But if they went down $5 on a $50 stock and then regained $5 or $10, you know you're not really making any money. What I mean is that you need to keep track to really know what your stock is doing. My thought is to be cautious. Don't rely on what anyone tells you. Do some investigating on your own before you start investing any money. If you do so before working with someone, you can at least be alert to some of the things in stocks or products they present, for comparison to their presentation.

I don't know of a fixed age or bracket that would be right or wrong for safe haven investments like annuities. It depends on people's needs. But that being said, probably between age 50 or 60 you need to start looking at annuities. That's the time you might start thinking more about preserving your capital, as opposed to earlier in life.

Along the way, I was fortunate to work for a major office supply company for 38 years. Before that, another company owned us, and each company had a stock savings plan. Once I got into management I would always recommend to people, especially young people, that they should take a portion of their earnings—automatically through payroll deduction—and start saving with stocks. That was because at the time, with both of these companies, you could buy their company stocks and they would match them. One of the companies matched 100 percent of what you bought and the other matched 50 percent, and it was great for saving at the time. For me, that really was the beginning of the investment world.

Today, however, not too many people can stay with a company as many years as I did, which I think is due to the way the jobs are moving overseas. So, when you start thinking about retirement, in your 50s or 60s, take some of the money you and your family feel you would need for the future, and put it in a safe place—because, these days, you never know what will happen with any company.

I took my pension out of the company and put part of it into the annuity. If I'd stayed with the pension, I would have gotten x-amount per month until I died, which would have been fine for me, but that would have been the end. What about my family? My thought was that if I could preserve that money and have it grow a bit, then when I did pass away there might be something left, which I could leave to my heirs. That's one of a couple of reasons why I went with the annuity up front.

When I converted my pension to the annuity, I was 63. I was lucky to have a pension at all. My son works for the State of Rhode Island and will have a pension—although some state governments are moving away from pensions. My son-in-law has worked many different jobs and will not have a pension, so it's very important for a person in his situation to start saving soon, or they will face traumatic times.

Once you have some savings, you can go with the kind of annuity I have, for example, and stay with the 3 percent fixed earnings. Or, you can put a portion of it in things like convertible bonds to have an opportunity to earn a little more. Again, if the bond earnings go down, I still earn the (base) 3%, and that's the important lesson you need to learn about the way annuities work.

My annuity also had the flexibility to let me begin getting an income almost right away. A year or two after I put money into the annuity, I started taking the pay-offs, and I've been drawing it down ever since. I have maybe $200,000 left in that annuity account, and with the money I've been drawing out, I probably have about eight years left at the current rate of income I receive. I've been using the draw-down provision for living expenses, using other muni-bond investments to accumulate value as they build to maturity. From the bonds, I take one lump sum each year, put it into a checking account and draw off that monthly.

Municipal bonds are another hidden subject you rarely hear financial experts talk about. They're kind of a hidden subject that can work with relative safety. Yet with municipal bonds, you have to be careful as well. Choose the best bonds; mine are triple-A insured. You can make more money on lesser rated bonds. With the better bonds you might make less money, but you can also rest more comfortably.

For example, right now my bonds are earning only about 3%, but keep in mind that I'm not in the market to buy anyway. Of the bonds I bought a few years ago, I'm getting an average of 4.5 to 5%, which is comparatively excellent during the times we're in. Yet, there are other things to consider: Many of my bonds were issued by the State of Rhode Island and they'll be free of state taxes for a period time. I have to pay federal taxes on earnings, of course, and I have to pay state taxes on other earnings. I also have bonds from the State of Florida and other places, but you have to keep in mind that they all fluctuate. However, if you stay in until maturity, you're at least going to get your money back.

Again, I've done a lot of homework, bought the bonds individually, myself, and started my own (bond) fund. I must have maybe 15 or more bonds today. Back when I had money, years ago, I was always trying to buy in $10,000 denominations or more. So I don't have a big investment in any one bond. I'm still diversified in my bond fund because they do carry risk. If something does happen, I have relative safety in diversity among many different bonds, and I do confer with a financial planner from time to time for occasional advice. But again, I track the progress of each bond on my own, and I do it often. Again, I choose only triple-A insured bonds so I can pretty much go it alone.

I say this because, although I don't begrudge anybody getting into the financial profession, you've got to be careful about going with any kind of broker, advisor or financial planner. There will be another downturn sometime. If you're reading this and we've had another one since the Crash of 2008, there will be another coming up, believe me. You have to do your own work to stay afloat.

Meanwhile, market and economic globalization is something we didn't have when I was younger, something old financial strategies didn't seem to take into account, even up to the 2008 crash. Back then, one country didn't have as drastic an effect on another, financially, but so many people are investing all over the world these days.

It's awfully scary to me—potentially what can happen with global economies, deficits, potential market problems. I think our leadership feels the same thing behind the scenes. President (GW) Bush favored a resolution from Congress that would require annuities for seniors. Obama said the same kind of thing, but turned around and talked about robbing our Social Security surplus to pay off the bailout deficit. Therefore, I think one of the better organizations we have now, like it or not, is the Tea Party because they let Congress know that the public can affect policy.

Where it will all lead, I don't know. Because of the way I've invested, I'm pretty much living the way I always have, the way I'm used to. I was only 59 when I retired and it was the beginning of the time when they gave out a pretty good package for people to retire. I got one of those packages so I've been retired for quite a while. Along with my other investments, I've been living the lifestyle we'd been living before. We really didn't have to change anything, although I've slowed down quite a bit since a hip replacement, and my wife was ill for a few years.

Before that we liked to travel. We went to a number of different countries—Portugal, Sweden, Germany. We loved to travel at the time but you have to adjust: Right now I'm living at home and taking care of the cats; we have about eight cats because my wife had them, I inherited them and they're all doing well.

On the other hand, I just got clearance after hip surgery to do anything I want to do. I probably won't be traveling as far but I'm cleared to go on airplanes or travel by car, so who knows? The new hip replacement procedures are fantastic; I was in the hospital for only two days, came home, went into physical therapy and was good to go after only four weeks. It's amazing how far we've come with medical care since I was a younger man.

One place I really want to return to is Medjugorje, Croatia (Dalmatia), where the miracle sightings of the Virgin Mary have occurred. I've been there four times, including once with my wife, and I'm looking forward to going back, once again, with my daughter Deborah.

*   *   *

CHAPTER 10

A Pastor Tends His Flock of Investments . . . with Guarantees

Paul is a full-time pastor at 80 years old and still working. He likes to say that "we keep going; that's what we do," when referring to himself and wife Jean, 79, with whom he just celebrated their 59th wedding anniversary.

They have two surviving children born in 1953 and 1963 respectively (they lost a daughter to illness in 1979), and some of Paul's grandchildren attend pricey private schools while his adult children work through the post-recessionary economy.

Meanwhile, Paul continues to lead an interdenominational congregation in New London, Connecticut, while living in a small town nearby.

Paul will touch on certain aspects of his semi-retirement, but he also asked to talk about things we can do to lend a hand in the community, something I've felt compelled to increase in Paul's direction, in addition to the other charities and my own foundation.

I hope you enjoy Paul's wisdom and life perspective as a person still working and affecting his community at age 80! For some of us, the term "retirement" does not have to mean stopping altogether, or stopping at all. But he does use some important tools to ease the burden a bit, while doing important work for his grateful parish.

Best Wishes to Those in Working Retirements,

Dave Reindel

*   *   *

Reverend Paul:

When Dave Reindel came to our house for the first time, I had some money in different places although I'd never really been in the stock market. That was back in the 1970s and I went with Dave specifically because Dave likes annuities and I trusted him.

I was in the insurance business for 25 years before I went into the ministry and I used to sell annuities, myself, because I know what they can do.

I was also in a mutual fund made of all stock. But I wasn't comfortable with it and wanted out, and Dave was able to get me out of it. On the brink of the last crash, not only was Dave able to get me out of the mutual fund, he was able to put me into a plan that would allow me to recoup all my money. It was, like, a week or two later when the market really dropped.

We made the switch just before October, 2008. If we hadn't, I would have really lost a bundle, yet I didn't lose anything. The Lord kept telling me to get out, and the timing was perfect. I'm very grateful because I was able to save everything and now the annuities with Dave, and Social Security, are my sources of income.

Besides that, Dave has always been very kind to me. I don't call for an appointment, I just walk in and he and Janet have always been very patient, very helpful and very generous. In fact, I think they've given back all the money I've given them (at Reindel Advisory Solutions, in Mystic, CT.)

They've given generously to the church. I never said anything to him, but we were sitting, talking business one evening and Dave said, out of the blue, "Oh, here, before you go—he handed me an envelope—and there was a check for $10,000 in the envelope for our ministries—both the church and our prison ministry. What a blessing!

When I saw the check I cried, and thought, Whoa, is this incredible. On that note, I have to share the following story because the investment we made before October 2008, followed by David's gift, came at the end of a long personal journey that led us where we are today.

Back in 1978, our 20-year old daughter had been an exchange student in Finland, but something wasn't right so our doctor sent her down to the New Haven hospital. A doctor came back and said she had a rare lung disease and gave her one to five years to live. In six months she passed away, which was devastating, and we really wanted some answers. A woman came to town while Barbara, my daughter, was still alive and ministered, and had we known more than we did at that time, she might still be alive.

I say this because we went to a prayer meeting where Barbara got up, full of energy, and walked out after the meeting. In fact, she felt so good, she said she wanted to run out and I probably should have let her. Anyway, after the prayer meeting, we wanted some answers and did some research, which led us to a gentleman named Kenneth Hagin and his Bible school in Oklahoma.

There we found that part of God's covenant is healing. Psalm 103, for example, says that the Lord forgives all of our iniquities, heals our diseases *and delivers us from destruction.* In the New Testament it says that "Jesus took our infirmities and bore our sicknesses." Scripture, including 1 Peter 2:24, says that "by his stripes we were healed." So much is said about God's will being available for healing. A part of 3 John 2 says, "Beloved, above all things I wish that you prosper and be in health, even as your soul prospers." God wants his people to prosper and wants his people to be healthy. I now think, after the last recession, that his will might include financial health, but that's another story.

After going to Oklahoma, we started worshipping in our home. That's how my life-change really started. Now, we knew we could ask people to come over and have church, but that would have been proselytizing, so we just left the door open, thinking that if anybody showed up, we would just share what we were learning.

Without doing much more than that, two people came, then four people came, and by the end of the year I think we had around 500 people pass through the house. That was in 1978. At that time, we went to a Bible training center and camp meeting in Oklahoma and I talked with a pastor there who decided we had the makings of a church. His church offered to license us and watch our progress and he said that within a year, if things went well, they would offer to ordain me.

Soon after I was ordained, we had a visit from an Episcopal priest, a born-again, spirit-filled Jewish man who said he wanted to start Sunday night services at his church. He invited us to join him in taking turns preaching. He did one week, I did the next, and that's how I got started.

Today, who would have ever predicted that one of the people who helped save our retirement finances would also help the church in so many ways? Dave's money helped with church expenses, of course, but he also helped our Paid In Full prison ministry, which helps former prisoners—once they are released from prison—with food, clothing and a place to live. We also belong to an organization called COPE, for Coalition Of Prison Evangelists. Most of the people in COPE are ex-offenders and are probably the best Christians I know. They know that nothing else works to break the walls down like Jesus, and they are wonderful people. We probably have six or seven COPE members attend church on a regular basis now, and Dave indirectly helped make it possible.

Although Dave isn't an active member of our church, he says we shouldn't be surprised if he and Janet show up one day. While I'm still waiting to be surprised, they still keep helping us. At least once a year they send us a check for something and the Bible says, "Give and it shall be given unto you." The way David gives, I'm sure it must be part of his success.

I'm also sure that integrity leads to the kind of community reputation Dave enjoys, and what Dave is doing by giving to the community is what I tell my congregation: Don't be overly concerned about what is going on in the world, economically, because we're under God's economy, and God said, "He would supply all our needs according to His riches and glory." People need to believe that, and I think a lot of people have gotten hold of that, including myself. Dave's generosity and the way our investments were transformed before October, 2008, are part of God's promise.

Everything I had I had in mutual funds. I really had a lot of money in those funds. Now, at this point in time, I have just the annuities—four different annuities—that Dave got for me, and I'm collecting on all of them now. The one with the major amount of money that I started last year is good for 10 years. I told Dave that if, after 10 years, I'm still here at 90 and that annuity runs out, I'm moving in with him.

One of my annuities is called an Immediate Annuity, which involves the contribution of a single premium and the immediate payout of income. The others Dave put together were meant to cover a certain number of years—one in particular covers seven years, so I'm drawing on that—all I can say is that it's just really helpful to get the same amount of money every month.

Looking back, I was in my late 50s and we were heading into another recession, which is interesting because times are similar now. Because of my age, I was getting concerned. I looked at free-dinner invitations in the mail. I went to five or six different dinners where I was given information. But I was but not motivated to do anything.

Back then I also heard a lot of people say, "Don't put your money into annuities; they'll take your money out of play in the stock market." So, I went to see a financial advisor in town, who told me to put all sorts of things into the market, and that's the way things went until around 10 or 12 years ago, when I first connected with Dave, and I'm glad I did, especially after October, 2008.

I just think that David is doing a great service for his clients by helping them put stability in their financial future. It has been a big help for us, and I'm sure he will be as kind and thoughtful with his other clients as he has been to me.

His service is important because financial prosperity is, after all, part of God's will. Scriptural teachings about money and money management include *Deuteronomy 8-18*, which says that "God gives us the power to get wealth . . . whose covenant may be established." So people need to understand that God must be involved in what they're doing financially. In *Joshua 1-8* it says, "This Book of the Law (i.e., the word of God) shall not depart from your mouth, that you shall meditate in it day and night so that you may observe all that is written in it . . . then you will make your way prosperous and then you will have good success." *Malachi 3-10* is about tithing and *Luke 6-38* says, "Give and it shall be given to you in good measure, pressed down, shaken together and running over."

References to prosperity continue in *2 Chronicles 26*: "He sought God in the days of Zechariah who had understanding in the visions of God; as long as he sought the Lord, God made him prosper." Other references include *Isaiah 48-17*, and *3 John 2*, which says, "Beloved, I wish it above all things that you shall prosper and be in health, even as your soul prospers." *Proverbs 3* through 9 and 10 tell us to " . . . honor the Lord with your possessions and with the first fruits of all your increase so your barns will be filled with plenty, and your vats will overflow with new wine."

But we're also charged with being vigilant and I think annuities play a role in that. My son-in-law had a big income and a lot of money in the stock market, but he took a beating. Well, I didn't and I've felt very secure with annuities. I believe that it was a wise move on my part, with Dave's guidance, to get into the annuities I have now. All I can say is, so far, so good.

When I try to talk to my kids and grandchildren about retirement, I would certainly recommend that they have annuities as part of their portfolios. Both families have earned pretty decent incomes, and my older daughter and her husband are pretty savvy about investigating what they do with their money, but I think safety of principal and some kind of certainty about future income can make all the difference when you get to my age.

*   *   *

A New Generation of Solutions
From Dave Reindel:

Before moving on to our next guest, let me talk about some new strategies available. We have some great solutions and there are new ones coming about all the time.

Basically, with all the uncertainty out there, people want something with certainty in their lives and that's what we provide. That's the kind of planning we do. Using annuities, you have qualified money and non-qualified money with guarantees. We also have death benefit guarantees for your heirs. So everybody's situation is different. But the only way you can find out what works for you is to sit down and talk to us. I take the time because it's a time intensive situation. We work on solutions and the client who takes the time to work on solutions will end up in a better place.

I have over 700 clients now and their solutions fit their scenarios. They're happy people. I can open up my file drawer, which is essentially what I've done with this book, and every one of them will say we've been careful about the way we've tailored the right solution to their retirement.

There are some people I don't work with because there is no solution. I say no because some people have expectations that are too high. I say no to certain people because I know they aren't telling me everything they should be telling me.

So, I don't want just a client, I want a relationship. My clients call me about anything and everything. They ask me if they should buy a new car or lease one, or buy a new house, or sell or rent the old one, you name it. Should they do a reverse mortgage? Should the cash in an investment, give it to a child *and* do a reverse mortgage?

Life changes and my mantra is this: If you call me up with a question and my answer is more than three sentences, we're going to meet because I want to see eye-to-eye that you know what we're talking about. After that, I spend the time with my clients to make sure that as they go through life, we're there to help them with the changes that happen, to keep them in that somewhat secure position. This is because, with everything else going on, people still are nervous about inflation, they're nervous about the cost of heating oil when oil prices rise—they're nervous about so many things going on in the world.

We try to do the best we can because I know that if you live another five years, I can guarantee that things will be different.

The only solution is in the planning and we have the tools for that planning. Just starting the process is half of the game. People don't start due to ONE WORD: fear. They're afraid to face reality. They're afraid to talk to someone different. They're afraid that they've already made mistakes and they don't want to make them again. I've heard people say that after talking to people they trusted, their accountants, tax people, big name brokers and bankers, they really didn't get the kind of advice they needed and lost a fair amount of money. That's what they say.

For some people, I wonder if the advice they got wasn't good advice after all, especially if they were looking for risk-based information. Stock brokers talk about risk, tax people talk about reducing taxes from gains and losses, accountants take what you've already done and try to plan, based on the risk situation you have chosen for yourself! That's the point: the client took the risk. Sometimes they don't want any more risk, but I think a lot of people don't move because they're reluctant about moving from risk-oriented circles.

To really understand how it feels to MOVE OUT OF RISK for the rest of your life and put at least some, or most, of your assets into guaranteed income, you have to be willing to look forward and make the move. Too many people never do that and it's sad when I have to talk to somebody who waited too long. Don't be that way. Have an open mind and take a look at my solutions. That's why I've written this book, with the kind permission and cooperation of the people who have volunteered to share their stories.

Sometimes it helps to hear from someone besides another advisor or financial planner, a real person who learned how to rely on guaranteed income instead of risk. I say this now because I look at the stock market in the past year. Once again, it has been going up, up, up. People forget about the past. They think they have to jump in and speculate all over again to stay in the game, in a game that's all about risk.

You and I can't invest in these companies. The door is closed and the people on the inside make all the money, and I'm afraid that as more and more companies work like this—which was the way it was long ago, by the way—we're only going to be left with the shakier companies that have to go public to raise money. THOSE are the very companies that will cost you a huge chunk of your retirement portfolio, time and time again.

#

I'd like to add another brief comment to this chapter from a gentleman with much to say about our current state of both financial and political affairs.

Former U.S. Representative and former Senatorial candidate Rob Simmons has seen much in his travels, having talked to so many people around the northeast and nationwide.

I hope that what he says resonates with you as well as it did with me,

David Reindel

*   *   *

Rob Simmons:

I enjoyed reading Dave's last book, *Don't Die Broke*, because it deals with people like me—baby boomers who worked their whole life, and set aside money for their retirement.

We've been personally responsible, we've tried to do the right thing, we paid our bills and made our own investments. Then, wow, over a couple of years everything went south and it went south at a time when many of us had been thinking about retirement.

I had to talk to my wife around that time and I had to say, "I don't think we're going to be retiring anytime soon." Of course, I'm not going to retire, but I think the point of Dave's planning philosophy is important.

There are a lot of people out there like me who have worked their whole life, set money aside, paid for their homes, maybe sold the house and put it into an equity investment and lost. So now we're confronted about retirement, and, OF COURSE, the government will be there to take care of us, right? The government's going to do everything for us, right?

Wrong. What is the government really going to do?

After the crash, the government hit us with a health care plan that is going to cost $2 trillion and, at the same time, seniors that were on social security saw that there was no cola that year. Even though the cost of living goes up every year, the criteria for the cola was missing, so they didn't get one.

A lot of seniors I talk to are on Medicare, or about to go on Medicare, and under the new health care bill there are going to be cuts of almost $525 billion in Medicare. So my question about Medicare is that as we bring more people on Medicare, as we cut Medicare, is the level of service going to remain the same?

I would argue that now, more than ever, it's important for seniors—and those who are going to go into retirement—to take a close look at what their financial situation really is and get ready, because things have not been so good during the past couple of years. We have to take over our own finances. You really have to take what you have, start where you really are, and go forward and have contingency plans for changes sure to come.

A lot of people have a major investment in their home. My own biggest investment is in my home. I need a place to live and I don't plan to sell it. But let's say I decided to sell it because I wanted to take the money and plan for my retirement. The housing market isn't very good is it? So, how do you deal with somebody whose major asset is their home? Maybe they have equities that have vanished altogether. How do you deal with somebody like this?

We have a lot to think about at this time, after the Crash of 2008, especially as we look at a whole new set of rules in the new global economy, where inflation based on our massive national debt hasn't even begun to gather real momentum.

(Editor's note: Some of the comments above include excerpts from our "Don't Die Broke" radio show, which include aired segments that may be found on our web site: www.davidreindel.com.)

#

CHAPTER 11

A Cautious, Working Entrepreneur and Her Secret Plan

We'll call her "Sandra" and leave it at that, due to her own request to remain unnamed. Given the current climate of identity theft and because so many people pray on seniors in retirement these days, it was her preference to remain anonymous, but she has a good story to tell.

A client of mine since the summer of 2010, she is actively working while getting ready for retirement in a few years. As a one-time small business owner, part of her plan is to eventually retire, but like so many entrepreneurial people out there, she had no way of knowing whether or not she would ever be able to get there.

I've been able to help her see that she can retire, and with security.

At 60, Sandra has nice retirement portfolio, which we put into a fixed annuity package offering guaranteed income. Because Sandra is tired of running night and day to run her businesses, she wants to know exactly what she'll be getting in terms of income by the age 67. By then, she could decide to do just about anything she wants, whether it means staying in business part-time or going into retirement full-time.

Either way, I'm happy to have this hard-working, innovative entrepreneur for another perspective—because so many Americans in small business form the backbone of our economy. Unfortunately, as politicians love to praise the small-business entrepreneur, so many government policies—both state and federal—seem to work against them.

More than any other group, American entrepreneurs need a hand when it comes to their well-deserved years in a safe, secure retirement. So, take note, with my very best regards to all independent business owners.

David Reindel

*   *   *

"Sandra":

As a business owner, your income can fluctuate, and it can fluctuate a lot. Sometimes you feel like you're investing more into your business than you're getting out of it. Sometimes valuations of your business go up, and sometimes they go down. So, as a business owner it's a scary thought wondering if you will end up with enough money to ever retire.

Once you do manage to retire, will you ever run out of money? That's not a position I ever want to be in, so I think it's wonderful for people to have life situations leading to a fixed income that would support their accustomed lifestyle.

I was concerned that we would never be in that situation, but by working with David, we've come up with a plan that will allow us to retire—not only with the lifestyle we're accustomed to, but basically with enough to live on forever. And we will still have all the original money we invested, which can be passed on to inheritance. That, to me, is really exciting. It's just nice to know that you have that kind of cushion, enough that when you die you won't be broke, that when you die, nobody will have to pay for your funeral.

My husband is still working and hopefully will be able to keep working until he's 67. We also want to consider the futures of our three children and four grandchildren, but at 67, my husband and I will be getting a set amount a year. My yearly income will be greater than what it is currently, and in seven years it will suffice. It should keep up with inflation in the next few years and we will retire with a six-figure income.

During the crash of 2008, and over the course of our lives, we have definitely lost a ton of money, especially in oil and gas investments back in the 1980s. For reasons like that, over the course of time you start thinking that you may have a financial advisor that doesn't always give the best advice.

Over the past 40 years we've taken our fair share of hits. You have it in stocks, in mutual funds, in all sorts of things. No matter what kind of mix you have in a retirement plan like that, very few people came out of it without losing a bunch of money. My big concern was that I would never be able to retire with enough money without having to work all sorts of odd jobs, and yet still live comfortably. I knew the path we were on wasn't leading us down a road with a lot of certainties.

When you're younger you can take all sorts of risks. Today maybe I can still be a risk taker, but my husband is not a risk-taker. So when we received a post card from Dave about a meeting coming up, instead of tossing it in the circular file—like we usually do—we read this one and my husband and I decided to go. It really sparked both of our interests. We wanted to know a bit more, wondering if we had enough money to do what he was talking about.

So, we both read his book (*Don't Die Broke*) and I read it cover to cover. When we came back from a vacation, we went to Dave with a very organized pile of financial information—we already knew what our monthly budget was and all of that—so Dave just took the information, worked with it and came up with a plan of action. We reviewed the plan and decided that a guaranteed amount of earned interest and guaranteed preservation of principal is, in this day and age, pretty decent.

We liked the programs he chose so much that we proceeded to have him handle it all for us, and it has been a very nice situation. We closed out a lot of other investments through October and November, 2010, when everything was going up. We were able to sell at the highest the market's been in a long time and that was nice. But had we not had a plan, it would have been very easy to do nothing and hold on in the market a little bit longer. When you have a plan in action, you don't do that.

Now it's very convenient because we don't have to be watching the stock market. My husband has always tried to play around with the stocks a little bit, but you can't do that very well and succeed on a part-time basis. We no longer have to worry about that.

Things were doing fairly well over the 10 years before the crash, so you tend not to worry. You tend, as you're aging, not to worry because you have all these years ahead of you when you can still be saving. You make a good choice, you win, you make a bad choice and you lose. Then all of a sudden you wake up one day and you're 60 years old and you decide you don't want to run the rat race you've been running for the last 30 years. You have to come to a reality check and decide that maybe you need to be doing something proactive.

I think that some people wait too long. All sorts of people handle money in all sorts of ways. We set our goals and dreams differently, but unless your goals are written down on a sheet of paper, unless your goals have a deadline, it's all still a dream.

In the United States, people are dreamers more than goal makers and seekers. And a lot of Americans are more concerned about being taken care of by Uncle Sam than they are about taking care of themselves, which I find extremely sad.

I *know* our annuities will take care of us. The annuity has guaranteed income for life and it's indexed so as the market goes up it can improve, but the base rate will never go down. Basically, the insurance company guaranteed a base rate, yet it can improve (with the market) and that's the beauty of it. I think that more people need to realize that there are options like this out there. You don't have to have just huge sums of money; you really just need a good plan.

When we started with David, my first reaction was that we probably wouldn't even have enough money to invest in his kind of plan, and that it wouldn't really work, but it was very interesting to watch it all come together. David is really good at looking at a number of different factors, also understanding what different people want, what their expectations are. He wanted to know if this (annuity income) would be the only money would live on. Well, not necessarily because we still own some properties and other assets, but now we won't have to bank on that. I don't have to worry about the sale of joint-owned properties, things like that.

We had a variety of assets before the crash and we definitely took a hit during and before the crash. Everybody did. But then we had to face facts and ask ourselves where we would go from here. Again, I think that a lot of people dream and fantasize and as long as it's still in your mind and not written down, it's a dream. So, write it down. Develop a smart plan. If it's specific, measurable and attainable and has a time frame, it becomes a smart, attainable goal. If you don't have this kind of measurable goal, but instead you think you have it altogether upstairs in your brain, you don't know the difference between dreams and reality. In fact, I think so many people today are actually afraid to turn their dreams into reality.

As I've said, we worked with different kinds of planners in the past. So many times, when you're dealing with financial planners you hear a lot of "ifs." "If" this happens, "if" that happens, then maybe something might happen in a certain way. That's frustrating, and sometimes you can end up putting your money with people that—people who, in the long run, you feel that you hardly know. At one point, we were putting our money with a highly recommended financial planner that we weren't feeling very comfortable working with, nor were we comfortable with where he was investing our money.

Dave was different. He could show you a plan of action that didn't have a ton of "ifs". That was a first.

Over the course of the last 35 years, we've been with a bunch of people and you learn to look for warning signs. I can think of one situation with a certain financial planner where things changed radically in his office. He started downsizing his staff—a lot. He started smoking heavily, when he'd never smoked before. He was talking down some stocks that wouldn't necessarily be so bad. I don't know, you sometimes get the gut feeling that it's time to pull some assets out and put them somewhere else, and to get your advice from someone else. If things change with someone with whom you're dealing, you see changes in their personality. You sometimes have to follow your gut.

If this happens to you, go with it. Start thinking that you can go with someone better, someone who is really in it for you—because some financial people are really in it more for themselves. We all know they're being paid commissions, but you have to be prudent and watchful—not in denial—because people change over time.

We also moved across the country at one point, which led us to change how we were planning our finances. For a time, my husband thought he would dabble in the market, but either way, you need to get your financial options from someone you can trust. And when it came to David, I really hadn't had anybody do as much in-depth study of exactly how much I thought I might need in retirement. People can throw out all kinds of numbers, but it's important to actually look at your budget, see how much you're spending now, today, and carry that forward.

Then come changes in your life, which affect the reality of your plan. We moved from one economy in the mid-west to a new economy on the east coast, where living costs were different, which affects your budget. My husband's company was downsized at one point, so a lot of things affect your finances. You can only hope you make the right choices and follow the right directions and insights.

After the crash (of 2008), we knew it was time to just try and make the best of what we have, and we needed a real expert to help sort it all out. There are so many options with so many financial people, unless you're dealing with someone who is really well-educated in a specific area or field of finances, you will find that so many of them don't have a clue. They might have taken a couple of courses, they may have passed the tests, but in reality they may be only pushing certain products for certain people.

The beauty of dealing with someone like Dave is that he's independent, not owned by Smith Barney or Edward D. Jones, or TD Ameritrade. Still, you have to take matters into your own hands, at some point, and take a close look at where you are and with whom you are dealing. Unfortunately, it doesn't always seem pressing to face things that must be addressed, so you have to make it pressing. You have to set aside all the more immediate little crises in life and make some moves for your future.

I also think we need to pass this kind of thinking along to our children. Our young people are taught a lot about things they will probably never need to know much about, while missing important knowledge about things they'll need to know for the rest of their lives—and I mean how to handle money, how to invest money, and how to take care of the future. This also includes knowing how to take care of your body, which can really cost you lots of money if you don't. You need to know how to take care of your children and their mental, physical and psychological health.

Unfortunately, those things are not taught in school. So we have a big group of Americans who learn about money and health by osmosis—often from other people who are misinformed—even though money and health are some of the real, basic necessities for having a good life.

*   *   *

Details, Details . . . and the So-Called "Nominal" Everyday Risk
(from David Reindel)

I started thinking about things Sandra mentioned during our interview. She made a number of observations that hadn't occurred to me, including the necessity of protecting your health from Day One, which begins when we're young and carries onward into a successful retirement.

Then I thought about the normal and even nominal risks we all encounter in life, like the simple fact of being laid off, which is a fact of life today that wasn't so much of a factor 50 years ago, when many of our parents were able to methodically plan for cookie-cutter retirements. Oh, to have that cookie cutter back again. But the cookie cutter is no longer real.

After listening to Sandra, another element came to mind. Due to the sheer nature of her request for anonymity, I realized that so many other Americans feel the same way about exposure to a variety of risks. Risks other generations had no need to worry about. Looking at it in another light, they faced lots of risks we no longer fear, like polio and tuberculosis, and a host of on-the-job safety concerns now prohibited by law.

But the law in itself has become something of a risk, in its own right, and seniors in retirement need to be wary not only of identity theft but litigation, which is why I am pleased to introduce our next guest.

Lori Cataldi is a Personal Risk Manager with a major insurance carrier. As such, her day-to-day passion is the study of personal risk from all angles, and the discovery of ways to better avert that risk.

After covering a variety of different risks, we decided to highlight one or two areas most seniors tend to forget. Yet, without being fully covered against such risks, we often find ourselves facing the loss of everything we've worked so hard to gain for our retirement lifestyles.

One such risk involves the family car and the simple act of driving. This can be a very touchy subject for seniors as we age, especially for men, I think. How many times have you heard elderly people say, "I've been driving all my life, and I know what I'm doing"? By age 70, we've been masters of the open roads for more than 50 years.

To accept the fact that our reflexes, eyesight, medications and other factors can affect performance behind the wheel can be one of the toughest hurdles for some of us. Loss or limitation of driving privileges can be one of the more disturbing moments of passage in anyone's life. But the idea of losing everything we own is far more daunting.

As for risks other than those taken in the stock market, this short, but concise section of the book will hopefully give us all good reasons to take some time and review those "little" details in our insurance coverage. By now, you know me and my love of cars. After listening to the suggestions from Lori below, even I made a thorough review of my own policies.

I trust you will do the same.

—David Reindel

Lori Cataldi:

You might have a great estate plan, but how do we protect ourselves against lawsuits?

Reindel: Right, when driving a car it becomes a potential weapon. People come to my office and their lives have been changed, just because of what happened with a car.

I agree, Dave. One the big areas to be aware of is a hole in the family insurance program, especially when people haven't looked into a personal umbrella policy. The personal umbrella policy is designed to go over and above your auto and homeowners policies. It's basically going to protect you from a serious liability claim, which you unfortunately become responsible for, if you're at fault in an accident.

The umbrella policy provides a high limit of liability coverage and most holes in coverage occur when the insured doesn't have an umbrella at all—or, when the umbrella limit is not high enough to meet their current assets.

At my company, we look at your level of umbrella protection. We also look at the need for Excess Uninsured Motorist Coverage, which is additional protection for yourself, and it can be vital.

Not all umbrella insurance companies offer Excess Uninsured Motorist Coverage, so you need to ask, but if you're injured in an accident by an at-fault party—and the accident is not your fault—it covers you and your passengers if that at-fault party does not have adequate coverage for injuries, or if the at-fault party has no insurance at all, which happens these days.

Too many people overlook Excess Uninsured Motorist Coverage until it's too late. The claim will first start on your auto policy. Typical coverage will be $100,000 per person, $300,000 per accident, although it can go as low as $20,000 per person, $40,000 per accident. What I suggest is that you purchase at least the same amount of Uninsured Motorist Coverage on your auto policy as you do with your regular Bodily Injury limit.

If you are injured in an accident by an at-fault party, you would first collect money under your Uninsured Motorist Coverage on your auto policy. Then, once you exhaust that, the Excess Uninsured Motorist Coverage kicks in.

This type of coverage is important for people of all ages, not just seniors. For example, if you are ever permanently disabled and you're the sole bread-winner, your claim could be in very high figures, and that's exactly where this excess coverage becomes important. It replaces lifetime income, among other things, protecting the family against catastrophic financial loss. It can mean the difference between a good solution, and having your life turned upside down by somebody without insurance, which could wind up costing you millions.

Retirees need to think about this because, as we age, we become more susceptible to involvement in traffic accidents, even though we may not technically be at fault. Younger people sometimes react to slower moving traffic from time to time, which can lead to devastating mistakes—made by young people without adequate insurance coverage.

I had this happen to actual customers who were unfortunately killed in an accident. They were not at fault but thankfully we had this excess UM coverage in place so that survivors would have money for ongoing living expenses.

Reindel: I'd like to add that we're still in a recession when people in general, people of all ages, are letting go of their insurance, or reducing their coverage. Again, it's my responsibility to protect myself properly, which depends on my asset levels and lifestyle. It is certainly an area people need to be aware of, and I certainly think that people should not have their insurance coverage in a drawer and never look at it again. We need to review these things and make sure we have adequate coverage, and inspect rates. Maybe we can get a better rate someplace else. But here's another caution: I see advertising these days promoting a program allowing customers to design their own policies, which means that a lot of people are going to design the policy as cheaply as they can, rather than buy a policy with everything they need. It's like going to an electrician saying, "I'll fix this myself. You show me where to do it and let me put my finger in the electric socket." I'm not going to do that. I want a professional who understands the industry, who has a good company behind them. God forbid if you're killed;

that's life wrenching enough for your family. To have an economic burden on top of that just worsens the situation even more.

True, Dave, and the umbrella policy is so inexpensive. As an example, a $1 million umbrella policy can cost anywhere from $150 to $300 per year, so it's a no-brainer to include one in your insurance program.

Reindel: We're in a world where people are cutting back. We're in a world with a lot more cars. At least some states have forced teenagers to drive with limitations, instead of just starting out with five kids in the car, laughing, screaming, hollering, texting and everything else. I was driving in a convertible the other day and saw another car in the lane next to me being driven by a young girl. Through the steering wheel, she was texting and even though our top was down, and I was waving my arms to get her attention, she never saw me because she was so intent on her texting. She was not driving that car, which scares me. She could have so easily caused an accident . . . and she's out there driving around right now.

I hate to say it but there are lots of irresponsible people in the world who, on top of being irresponsible, have inadequate coverage. The two seem to go together, unfortunately. All of a sudden, they can turn our lives upside down because somebody failed to have adequate coverage.

Personally, I don't buy auto insurance to cover every little thing. I buy it for the large claim and go for the max, so I have large deductibles. I have money saved if something happens and I'd rather have a large deductible to be able to afford an umbrella policy than the other way around—to expect the insurance company to pay from Dollar One. That's not what auto policies are designed for. Your insurance is designed for a major loss. If I total a car, my insurance is going to cover it. But if I have a fender-bender and it costs a couple of hundred dollars, I pay it out of my pocket.

The other part is that I don't want the insurance company to raise my rates because of every little thing that happens. They share information on claims. We even have to have good credit to get good policies. There are so many things that affect premiums already, so it's not like it used to be. When I was in the auto policy business, we never checked credit reports and now the details abound beyond that. We all need to make sure we're diligent, and you need an insurance professional you can call when things happen.

(Editor's note: Some of the comments above include excerpts from our "Don't Die Broke" radio show, which include aired segments that may be found on our web site: www.davidreindel.com.)

#

Not All Annuities are Alike:
Cautious Comments about Variable Annuities

Speaking of risk, a certain type of annuity can put your assets at risk and is often the culprit when media people mistakenly criticize annuities as a whole. I'm talking about the Variable Annuity, which isn't without options to mitigate risk, as my next guest and chief tax strategist Nick Stovall explains.

Nick talks about "the upside of being down" and variable annuities, while addressing numerous tax issues that put unnecessary risk in your portfolio.

—David Reindel

*   *   *

Nick Stovall:

I wrote a white paper called "The Upside of Being Down," which talks about variable annuities. A lot of people out there are under water with variable annuities. When I say "underwater," I mean their annuities are worth less than what they've paid into them.

So, what do we do with an underwater variable annuity? I get lots of calls from clients all over the country who have lost money from variable annuities and lost confidence in this kind of product altogether. So, what do you do with this kind of loss? Do you just cash out and walk away? Is there any benefit in that?

What we did was summarize tax perspectives around the variable annuity, both in recognition of income but, when sitting on this type of loss, looking for any upside.

Loss in this situation might be taken as an itemized deduction on your tax returns. That's very good news. The only catch is that you have to fully surrender the variable annuity and you have to have income to offset the loss. If you don't have income, there are some things we can do to offset that loss just the same, so that you're not stuck in this type of losing proposition.

For the above, we often use a Miscellaneous Itemized Deduction, which is subject to the 2 percent floor of your Adjusted Gross Income. What that means is that if your AGI is $100,000 and 2 percent of that is $2,000, that first $2,000 of the loss on your variable annuity would not be deductible. Using this model, if you've had a $10,000 loss, you'd only be able to deduct $8,000, but that's a significant amount, and we might structure that deduction to take advantage of a tax situation.

If you have this type of loss, and you have a potential use for it, we need to know to look at your overall tax structure because, for example, we don't want to be subject to the AMT, otherwise known as the Alternative Minimum Tax. A lot of people ask about the AMT and I sum it up saying, "It's bad." For that reason, if this Miscellaneous Itemized Deduction causes you to become subject to AMT, or if you didn't have the income to offset it, it's non-refundable so you're going to lose the deduction.

We don't want that, so we would need to take a deeper look at your overall tax perspective and make sure it's still a good thing. On the surface, it looks great, but is it great for you today?

Reindel: A lot of people surrender annuity accounts or make other changes without looking at the tax implications. You must look at everything in advance, and from all angles, regarding taxes. If there are ways to use tax advantages, we're going to use them, but you need a professional to sort things out ahead of time.

Right, Dave, and here's a misconception. When sitting on a variable annuity, some people think that if they take the loss it will be a capital loss. They think that since they don't have any capital gains it means they can only offset $3,000. Fortunately, it's not a capital asset so it's not capital loss. These losses are deductible against ordinary income because you take it out as ordinary income, so it's not a capital gain.

If you don't have the income to offset it, what are your options? This plays into a couple of areas. Take Roth conversions: The biggest thing keeping us back from Roth conversions today is that people don't want to pay the tax out of pocket. Understandable, but if you had a variable annuity and had a loss, you could take the loss and convert the exact amount of your deductible loss from your traditional IRA to your Roth IRA, creating income. Therefore you would have a zero out-of-pocket Roth conversion. That's very exciting. The Roth IRA is the second-best gift Congress has ever given us.

Outside of insurance, including life insurance, the Roth IRA is about the only way you are going to get tax-free income. So if you're down on your variable, there are some things you can do to get out of the variable, make some tax savings, and not suffer from surrender charges.

Reindel: I had one person who was so upset with his variable account, before he even called me he took a surrender charge because he thought it was something it wasn't. He thought he had no other option other than just surrender the policy and put the remaining assets into an IRA CD. This is a good example of a time to avoid panic. If he had called us, we would have had some time to point out some tax advantages.

(Editor's note: Some of the comments above include excerpts from our "Don't Die Broke" radio show, which include aired segments that may be found on our web site: www.davidreindel.com.)

\#

CHAPTER 12

Taking Care of Business at Home

... How to Give Back

I'm going to get a little personal, here and introduce you to someone very special to me.

I don't know how I can ever repay the person I'm about to introduce to you. He taught me so many valuable life lessons, including my love of automobiles. But he also taught me about having personal values and integrity. He taught me about the truly important things in life, which have nothing to do with money.

The man you are about to meet is my father. Now living in Rhode Island, he is a former master carpenter, construction superintendent and member of the carpenters' union in New Britain, Connecticut. You may not know about the carpentry profession, but it is difficult to get to this level. It takes hard work, expertise and the ability to know how to inspire teams, how to be a leader.

That's my Dad. But when it came to finances and retirement savings, I was able to offer him, and my mother, all the expertise I have, which made a difference in the way they both enjoy retirement today.

At 81, Dad loves to watch me drive up in my latest acquisition, whether it's a new car or something my friend Wayne Carini suggests. More importantly, Dad and Mom enjoy the home they live in and other perks made available through some of my Eight Golden Rules of a Successful Retirement.

—David Reindel

*   *   *

Dave's Dad:

I have to thank my son, David, for helping us enjoy a good retirement. He had me turn over investments into annuities, helped financially when I sold my house, and generally helped with my retirement process because I didn't know where to turn.

I retired at 65, but at 70, I had David look at my financial status. At the time, my wife and I had a three-story family house I couldn't afford. We had relatives on every floor: Mother on one floor, a mother-in-law on the other floor, the house wasn't quite paid off and we could have had renters, but it's tough to rent to moms.

So, David helped me financially, took my CDs and IRAs and put me into an annuity that gave me a better percentage of interest, which helped us out financially, believe me. We would never have been able to make it otherwise.

We sold the old house and moved to the new one we live in now. Between myself and David, who helped back me to buy the new house, we were able to do it. On the other hand, I've been a carpenter ever since I could put the spoon down and lift a hammer, so I've always helped David with his home renovations. We've had a long, great relationship.

Money wise, the annuities have made more interest than anything else, more than the bank CDs and IRAs, especially. A lot of people my age get stuck in their ways, but we have one annuity bringing in $200 a month just to help with groceries. Another annuity brings in $2,000, but the difference is that those annuities are continuing to make good interest, between 5-1/2 and 6 percent—try that with a CD these days. So, we're doing well with those, plus my pension from the carpenters' union.

David also pays our household expenses, from house payments to utilities. He is a very thoughtful son—let me put it that way. Even way back, as he does today, he would go to the nearest grocery and come in the house with bags of different meats and things, always very thoughtful.

So, we're living comfortably but we wouldn't have been able to do it without David, and now we're in a very nice home in a nice area of town, in a home originally built by Better Homes and Gardens. When this house was built, the newspapers kept up on the building process as it was being built. It's a ranch-style home with cathedral ceilings, post and beam construction, floor to ceiling windows, a 10-foot-wide fireplace with a grill built into the fireplace, two bedrooms, two baths, and an attached garage on a wooded acre of land.

David has given us a life we wouldn't have, I don't think, without his help. These days we're into auto racing, sports in general, football, basketball. We're now going to a lot of University of Connecticut men's and women's basketball games, and I still enjoy cars.

I've had nice cars since I was a kid: a Pontiac Grand Prix, a Buick Park Avenue, a Chrysler Cordova. Every five years I bought a new car and kept it in showroom condition—as neat and clean as possible and David always admired that.

Now he has antique cars, which are very nice, and he's tied up with car investments with Wayne Carini. I mean, he's very serious about his cars. He had a three car garage and added another two car garage to his house where he's had a Bentley, a Ferrari, an Aston Martin like the one used in the James Bond movies. You would be amazed by some of the Sundays when he would come over as we watched from our kitchen window. I'd see this amazing car coming up the road and suddenly swing into our driveway with David behind the wheel.

But it all goes back to his first car, a small MG sports car, as I recall, which he bought when he worked at a shoe store. Around the same time he was going to college and was on the dean's list two or three years in a row. He was also in the Civil Air Patrol and—by appointment of a congressmen—was nominated to go to the U.S. Air Force Academy. He was intent on learning to fly, but because of an eye refraction he was unable to fly with the Air Force. When he did get out of college, he went to work for an insurance company, and that's where all of this really began. He did really well for the company. When he wanted a little more money, he decided to go out on his own with Casualty and Life insurance, had several offices and did really well with all of them.

From there he went into bigger things, now Reindel Advisory Solutions, and then he got tied up with Fran Tarkenton, who became his close friend.

It all began way back and I knew David had something special going. I remember one thing in particular: With some kids, you would have to make them do their homework, and they give you a hard time. But David was different. For one thing, he wouldn't do his homework at night and he had a good reason. He said that if he did his homework at night, he would go to bed, get up in the morning and forget what he'd been studying at night. So, he would get up at 5:00 or 6:00 in the morning and do his homework, and he was very, very smart. He always did the very best at everything.

Another difference between David and other kids his age was the way he would never come to me and ask for money for this or that. David would always work something out to get the money he wanted. To earn money, he always had paper routes. At one point, he had two routes. He would go out in the snow to deliver the Sunday paper and it all went on from there.

Above all that, David is an honest person, that's for sure. He will try to help people in any way possible, just to help them along. He has given money to individual people who were down and out, along with a lot of charities; he always spent a lot of time just helping people, even if they weren't going to use him for his business advice.

In my experience, if you want to succeed in retirement, listen to Dave Reindel. He is one of the finest in his business. Listening to his radio program on Sundays, people call in to tell how David helped them with their finances.

David is quite a guy and there's nobody prouder than my wife and I.

* * *

"RETIREMENT" $$ vs. "INVESTMENT" $$
by David Reindel

Not everyone has the ability to provide the kind of support I like to give my parents in retirement. So many people would like to, but given lack the means, especially after the Crash of 2008, we do what we can. Yet, I want to let everyone know that a safe, secure retirement portfolio can be had without a great deal of financial knowledge.

All you need to start with are a few basic principles, which I call The Eight Golden Rules to A Successful Retirement, and they all begin with one, simple idea:

"Those who don't learn from history are destined to repeat it."

Coming out of the recent recession, we can dwell on negative memories and market losses, but there are reasons to be positive. Yet, you can't just do this with a happy face, you need a plan.

Taking control and knowing the difference is again talking to somebody who understands the difference, somebody who won't tell you what you want to hear but will tell you what you need to do.

The reality is that in this world, after the changes that have taken place since 2008 and even 2001, we're living in a New Financial Normal. In this new reality, you have to take control of your money and protect what you have so you will have it for a long time. Part of that scenario is in knowing the difference between "investment" money and "retirement" money. It's a simple concept that people often fail to grasp, but that's where it all begins, and the good news is that you can have both.

Develop different strategies for investment money and retirement money. Take your retirement money off the table and out of the casino, stay away from what happened in October, 2008. Learn a new thing, which is all about Reliability of Income, or ROI, and that's what I preach. To say there's the potential of a little liability out there is an understatement. At one point last year, the market suddenly dropped 1,000 points in a two-to-five minute period, basically due to a glitch in electronic trading.

You bet we have potential liability out there.

Today, investing is a different ball game. John Vogel from Vanguard recently said that "our corporate stewards have sold projections based on financial engineering driven by the assumption of massive risk, and the folly of short-term speculation has replaced the wisdom of long-term investing." It's a rent-a-stock system today. Not the old Warren Buffet buy-and-hold quality of management market share that determines how well a certain share or company competes.

It doesn't seem to fit the equation anymore, and the new paradigm seems to be holding true for mutual funds as well. Roughly 70 percent of the volume on all exchanges seemed to be coming from hedge funds, at one point, and they make their money on volatility. They don't care who owns the stock. They care about taking care of their customers, which would be pension funds, municipalities, and governments like Greece and the UK. That's who they're concerned about.

Here's another illustration from the *Wall Street Journal* and a very successful firm known for "fast trading," which is what accelerated the problem during the famous May 6, 2010, 1,000-point drop. According to the *Journal,* " . . . Often holding stocks and futures for only minutes or seconds, computer servers provide the horsepower that stand in several rows of metal cages in three consecutive rooms the size of tennis courts." Something like that. The lesson being that this one company, alone, employed 90 PhDs, including experts in quantum physics and artificial intelligence. The company had computer servers from Austin, Texas, to Kansas City, to Red Bank, New Jersey. All over the place and trading in microseconds, which is what can drive market volatility.

This is what individual market investors are up against, along with the basic reality of a unified global economy. We all know what's going on in Greece, and you may be wondering how that would affect you. Why should we worry about what's going on over there? Because we're all trading amongst ourselves, from nation to nation in overseas investments, stocks, you name it. When one nation pulls a group of others into the tank, it can easily affect the rest of us. It's more complicated than that, but it's a fact.

I'm all for taking a little risk, if someone is dying to get in the game and risk losing money for the fun of it. People packed into tour busses do that every day in Atlantic City and Las Vegas. I'm just saying take the "investment" risk if you have your "retirement" money locked into safe avenues of real income.

*   *   *

The following concept comes from my radio show, which I hosted on Sunday mornings at 9:00 am on WXLM from New London, Connecticut. We call it . . .

"ONE SIZE DOES NOT FIT ALL"

I say this often: Solutions are different for everybody and the right one for you depends upon your needs. But these two clients show just how diverse those wants and needs can be:

I get clients from all over the country who have read my book *Don't Die Broke*. One is from California, and he's the CFO of a major, major corporation. He's sharp as a tack and I was excited to talk to him because he understands math and the value of income guarantees and predictability.

Recently, he bought an annuity from somebody else and wanted me to analyze the product. For his solution, the parts in the product contract are applicable to everything he worries about. It's a California product, by the way, and when he bought it, the contract provided a 12 percent bonus and an 8 percent earnings guarantee for 10 years. Sounds great, but remember that all products in the income-planning world are different. I mention this product, which was fine when he bought it, and apply it to different situations. Maybe the product has high surrender fees, which account for the 12 percent bonus as an offset to the fees. It all points to one fact in the annuity market today. We have lots of ongoing innovation to look at, even in a recessionary economy.

A new product will soon be introduced that will benefit people who want to do some income planning but leave a substantial amount of money to heirs. It basically offers 4 percent growth for a death benefit. You can take that much out and leave the principal for your heirs. Again, there's so much stuff going on in the market today, I don't know what someone will need until I sit down with them, but we never seem to have a "One Size Fits All Situation."

I also have a client who is a well-known scientist in her late 40s. Every time she calls, she reads my book before she calls me, in its entirety. She's a Brainiac who has read *Don't Die Broke* five times already, and every time she re-reads it, she comes up with more solutions for herself. So, we take the tools we have and work with them again, but the same questions endure: How much money do you need, where is the income going to come from? Will it come from Social Security?

For most people Social Security will be the only way. There may or may not be a pension, and some 401ks should go into IRAs, but each situation demands a different set of solutions.

I talked to a client today who had Non-Qualified money, which simply means it's is non-IRA money. We can do income planning with that money with better taxation, and we can give him income with fewer taxes. Do you think taxes will be important?

Taxes are obviously going to go up eventually. We have a big debate about it now, but in my opinion our economy is falling down around us and we'll eventually need to raise taxes to eat up some of the looming deficit. But what really disturbs me is the emotional denial we seem to love to carry around, a state of denial we need to avoid in order to demand results for our economy. Meanwhile, all you hear on the news are things like the controversy over building a mosque near Ground Zero in New York. Give me a break. We have major, major problems in this country. I don't care about Lindsey Lohan's rehab problem and I don't care about the mosque. What I do care about are jobs, taxes, the things that matter: Like, how are we going to keep jobs inside this country?

Instead, we get diverted because, in my opinion, higher ups want to draw attention away from reality, away from what's really going on. I see people who are scared and uncertain, and this paves an unhealthy path to more market volatility, more economic upheaval and more need for reliable retirement income than ever before—because retirees no longer have the time to wade through the muck of risk and wait for recovery.

We try to plan. Even if it's an imperfect plan, it's a plan. A client I have is talking about a reverse mortgage, which isn't perfect. I wish he hadn't bought such a big house, but he has honed his budget to meet the lower income expectation for that kind of plan. He didn't fund the income plan the way he should've, but he came in today and we're working as a team. In short, I may not like what you've done, but I don't preach, I try to fix situations. Only you decide whether it's going to be good for you or not, but when we get a plan to a point that works, it's exciting.

Another client came to a seminar five years ago and told me he was not ready to make any decisions but that he had to have guarantees and to have growth in the market. I couldn't work it both ways. After five years and the last crash, he came back and said he'd seen no growth. He was finally ready for some serious income planning.

That's where we really are today. You can listen to all the news pundits and media analysts out there, who talk up this or that in the market, but only 6 percent of all stock mutual funds were left standing in the black between 2008 and 2009. Six percent!

One of the major hedge fund managers just got out of the business. He'd had a great run but recently said, "I can't do it anymore," and he's in the middle of the equities market. I mean, if this man can't figure it out, what am I going to come up with? This is why my kind of planning thrives on the coattails of all of the above; we're sick of losing principal.

We want to protect what we have and that protection comes in a lot of forms. I talk about money protection, lifestyle, documents, the long-term care issue, passing money on to heirs, meeting with clients, beneficiaries—you have to make sure all things are present and accounted for.

A lot of people in their 70s and older are still healthy and they may live a long, extended life. When I do planning I look at the life span of a husband and wife, and I look at the plan for both—to make sure there will be enough to live on, and live well, with as little disruption as possible.

That's the new reality!

On that score, I would like to introduce another client who has ridden out the recessionary storm while following my advice. For the purposes of safeguarding his identity, we'll call him "Henry."

He is 70 and living well in a suburb of Westerly, Rhode Island, and he has been working with me for about seven years, which places our relationship before the crash, which really paid off for Henry, as you will see.

The happy ending-in-advance to Henry's story is that he is married and living the good life in retirement. They have some discretionary income and are not struggling to live. In fact, they like to travel and go on cruises. They've been to Puerto Rico and the Bahamas and they have security in retirement. Henry has set up a will and Power of Attorney, which I advocate for all of my clients, so he can sit back and enjoy life beyond the workplace, making every one of his retirement years as carefree as possible.

His story involves what many of us consider "safe" company investment plans, which our employers offer during our working years. Henry was wise enough to see through all that, which eventually brought him to me, but I'll let Henry take it from here:

Henry:

I worked at Electric Boat with General Dynamics for 43 years and rose to become manager of my department. Being retired, I was looking for a good retirement plan for my life savings and after attending many retirement seminars, I was never satisfied with the presentations. Some lacked clarity. Some presenters said that when they invested your money they would get a good return for you. But they also warned that, if working with them, you had to be ready to accept a loss of your money if the stock market did poorly—which it definitely would in a few, short years!

Then I discovered Dave Reindel.

I attended the last of a series of Dave's seminars, which he presented in 2005, and I was impressed by his honesty and the kind of program he presented. His program was different than the rest: Dave stated that I would never lose any of my retirement money on his investment strategies, so I was definitely interested in what he had to say!

David would propose annuities from several insurance companies including Lincoln Insurance, Aviva and Great American Insurance. At the time, I had all my money in the General Dynamics SSIP Plan and I wasn't getting a great return—maybe around 1.5 percent—which had drawn me to attend Dave's insurance seminars. I'd heard that I could get a better return on my investments.

I was generally invested in General Dynamics' fixed-income program, which was protected, not directly related to the stock market. However, there were other options offering the potential of higher returns, including the General Dynamics stock market options program, where you could make up to 10 percent returns—or so they said at the time.

The problem with the company stock options program was risk. I could have lost money if problems developed with the stock option program, which could have easily happened during the last recession, starting in 2008. Although I was getting a low percentage of income/return in the fixed income program, I wouldn't have lost money due to stock market fluctuations.

Yet, I wanted to get a little more money from income without depleting the balance of my principal, and while most insurance plans at the time offered slightly more than banks, they didn't offer much more.

Then I took a good look at what Dave was offering. I liked what I saw and transferred a substantial amount of the SSIP funds into an annuity I was able to purchase through David, which is where I am today. The plan fluctuates, offering earnings between 6 and 8 percent, but even back then I started getting 6 percent right away. Through Dave, I now I get up to 8 percent for income purposes, and I get it without risking my principal balance!

As a lot of people know by now, this type of annuity lets investors get a certain percentage of whatever the insurance company makes in profit from its own investments. There are other details, but what I really care about are the reports I get from David and the insurance companies showing that I'm getting 6, 7 and sometimes even 8 percent. Banks don't pay that, do they?

This year, I might even get 10 percent on the annuities! And I'm looking at that without having to risk principal, so you can see why I'm sure David's investment strategies have been superior to the rest. I mean, way back when, some financial people were even proposing reverse mortgages and a lot of other radical ideas, which I didn't want to go do. Needless to say, with David I've been very satisfied.

As for my overall retirement plan, I have approximately 65 percent of my retirement with David and 35 percent remaining in the old fixed income program with General Dynamics. I can leave the rest of my money with General Dynamics for the rest of my life, and I may do that because I believe in keeping my money in more than one basket.

The General Dynamics stock option program is still a good one because for every dollar you invest, they will give you one dollar's worth of their stock, which sounds good at first—I took 100 percent of the General Dynamic stock option at one time—but as I got closer to retirement, I kept converting it to the company's fixed income program in order to get out of the stock market itself, and I'm glad I did.

Believe it or not, the General Dynamic stock investment program was supposed to give you 7 percent to 8 percent returns, but it was invested in the market and I wasn't comfortable with that. With David's program, I repeat: You get essentially the same return without the risk. David was able to increase my income over what I was getting from General Dynamics and I'm comfortable with that income because my money is safe. He also set up a monthly income fund from the annuities I got through him—to help me with retirement expenses; his plan has given me a good retirement supplement income. What more could you want?

All I can say is that I have been a client of David's for six years—straight through the recession—and I have never lost money I've invested with David. During the recent recession, not only did I never lose any money under David's guidance, David was always ready to give me prompt service when I needed it. And when I needed more retirement income, David adjusted the investment so I could have more money in a timely manner—we've had several meetings with David regarding changes in my investments and he was always there with the answers.

David's quick response to questions always comes in handy. For example, I recently turned 70-1/2 and at this age, federal laws state that you must withdraw a certain percentage of your protected investments, IRAs, etc., for tax purposes. If, for example, you have protected income like the SSIP from General Dynamics, they deduct the money from your paycheck through the years without taking any income tax from your check, so you can put it away and build x-amount of dollars. But when you turn 70-1/2, the government becomes nervous because you have a lot of (untaxed) money tied up in savings, so they require you to draw out the money and pay up.

I have two plans and we had to total up the two and pay tax/interest on both. Here again, David and his wife, Janet, helped me determine and satisfy the required amount to be withdrawn and we satisfied the government requirements in a timely manner. Without help from Dave and Janet, it would have been a more difficult process for me, alone, which is one more reason why I am a truly satisfied customer of David Reindel.

In summation, after the Great Recession gripped the nation, Henry had no worries: "I felt relieved," he said. "All my income was secure, I'd planned on it. So, the recession had no effect on me at all. I tried to warn my friends about the coming recession and that there were ways to avoid risk in the market, but a lot of them wouldn't listen. A lot of them stayed with the General Dynamics (stock program) and they lost their shirt."

> *I couldn't have said it better myself. Company option plans and other "benefits" can sound awfully convenient, and secure, but nothing is more secure than guaranteed principle. If you are currently employed and enrolled in your company's investment programs, you might consider out-of-the-box options as you near retirement.*

> *Now let's move on and look at an investor on the other end of the spectrum.*

> *—David Reindel*

CHAPTER 13

A Crash Survivor Goes "Public"

Many of you have heard the following guest on the air with me. He is a virtual, walking-talking wealth of information about the economy, politics, social trends, you name it.

His name is Richard and he is the tireless researcher. If you are one of the many thousands who tune into my weekly broadcast, you might have heard his voice.

But here's the secret we're about to reveal. Unless you have read my book to this point, you would never know that Richard is also one of my clients. Richard came to me not so long ago after losing heavily during the crash of '08. As he will tell you very shortly, he wasn't sure if he would ever be able to retire or not. He wasn't sure what he would do at all, which makes his survival story perhaps one of the most poignant in the book.

Even more interesting to me is the fact that Richard was one of those high-powered corporate executives who had every kind of investment resource at his fingertips. Along with those resources, he was much more knowledgeable about how to invest in the market than most of us.

I also know that Richard was the kind of investor who would leverage his investment risk with the utmost caution. He carefully researched any potential investment in advance, before buying anything in the equities market, and he had some of the best advice the equity industry could offer. He was no fly-by-night investor, believe me. Richard was the real deal.

Yet, Richard still lost major portions of his retirement portfolio. So, any one reading this book who might feel even slightly embarrassed about suffering losses during the crash, or during the past decade, take heart. You and millions of others like you are in very good, conscientious company. You must also know that we were able to work out a plan for Richard. His story has a happy ending.

Richard is now comfortably retired, at age 73, because he has a plan. He knows exactly how much income he will receive every month for the rest of his life, and because of this certainty, he has been able to adjust his monthly budget and he is living well as a result.

Through our plan, Richard discovered the power of peace of mind one can have with absolutely guaranteed principle and income. He has become such an advocate since the crash, sometimes I think he believes this stuff even more passionately than I do.

For that reason, and because Richard had so much astute knowledge, you are about to meet him in print in order to learn from his most compelling story.

While I know that you will enjoy what he has to say, I think you will gain much insight about the "why" behind the logic of having guaranteed income for life because, in the end, it really is not about the money. It's really all about having peace of mind.

After hearing from Richard, and after a few parting words of my own about fixed index annuities, my friend and business partner Fran Tarkenton will offer some riveting comments in the closing epilogue of this book, which I am sure you won't want to miss.

—*David Reindel*

*   *   *

Richard:

Many of the people tuning into David Reindel's radio show, and the people in his book, represent the real face of the investment world left standing after the Crash of 2008. We all have something in common and we call it "R.O.I."

My story speaks to the importance of the new definition of R.O.I. for all retirement candidates. R.O.I. is NOT a "return on investment." For us, it means RELIABILITY OF INCOME. Before 2008, I thought return on investment would deliver reliability of income. No more. For many of us, the first step in recovery from 2008 was to understand, accept and act on these two mutually exclusive sources of income.

We continue to hear all the numbers: Including the people who have stopped looking for work, we are really looking at 10 percent unemployment, another 14 million are under-employed, 4 million home foreclosures are pending, 30 percent of home owners owe more on their mortgages than their homes are worth. Most people lost 45 percent or more of their retirement income *twice* in the last ten years . . . once in 2001 and again in 2008. As many of us have had the new-normal economy imposed on us, we have implemented constructive adjustments. Some good things are coming out of all that pain.

People are saving 6 percent of their income. Before 2008, they were saving 1 percent. In spite of the devastating financial statistics imposed on so many families, necessity is the mother of invention . . . people are finding ways to save. Spending is out. Frugality is in. People are stringing barbed wire around their Reliability-Of-Income money and they are also making dramatic changes in their lifestyles . . . for example, no more eating out but grilling out instead. Today, they pay down their credit cards and use them sparingly. They use a debit card. They hang on to the ten-year-old Honda for ten more years. They send the kids to a state school instead of an Ivy League school. They make sure the homeowner's policy secures what really needs to be protected and no more. They re-evaluate health insurance plans and deductibles. They take a hard look at cable and phone bills and eliminate the bells and whistles. They reduce car travel and make sure their car insurance is reduced accordingly. They vacation close to home, turn the lights off and keep the heat and A/C manageable. They buy generics, not expensive brand names, and they watch for "value creep," or what I like to call "tag-ons." Tag-ons are added charges for what creditors consider new services to your contract, services you did not request. The airlines earned $22 billion in "tag-ons" last year, which included pretzels, seat selection, extra bags, etc.

Before 2008, there were many who had $1 million and now have $500,000. There are even more who had $500,000 and now have $250,000. There were a few who somehow held their assets together but not too many. This story of decline was as punishing to most hedge funds, equity partnerships and investment bankers as it was to the rest of us. In the new financial normal, there are many doubts about the wisdom of portfolio diversity, asset allocation, buy and hold.

I lost 40 percent of my assets in a diversified allocation of large cap, mid cap, small cap and emerging market mutual funds . . . all invested with reputable, highly regarded mutual fund companies. Not one of these sectors held its own in the tsunami of 2008.

David Reindel has a client who owns a web site/software business. Before 2008, he was offered $130 million for his business. It was recently sold for $30 million, which is still a very good number, but the nature of being human is to obsess over the loss, rather than take comfort in the ultimate gain. The former business owner is determined to keep this from happening again. His "Reliability Of Income" alarm went off. So, this client is buying an annuity to preserve principal and guarantee income. This client committed no errors of greed or run-away risk taking. He built a substantial business that lost considerable value in the crash, as did our investments. This successful entrepreneur is one of many offering a road map for the management of our different financial circumstances, which leads to an achievable financial future.

In order to identify and act on Reliability-Of-Income money and "return-on-investment" money, planning is necessary. Before 2008, only 20 percent of us sought professional financial planning advice. Today, about

70 percent rely on a reliable, reputable, knowledgeable and experienced retirement planner, with a record of success and solid references.

We are not talking about "product pushers" who have a "flavor-of-the-month" new product to sell and a sales quota to meet. Because the markets were so kind to many of us over the years, we did not see the risky investment behavior that was so forcefully made clear to us in 2008, and neither did most stock brokers, accountants and bankers. We lived in a world of investment self-hypnosis because we expected Reliability-Of-Income from investments that became very, very risky during the gathering momentum of the recession. And the cheerleading to buy more continued from our financial pundits who made their money on the certainty of the next new financial breakthrough product . . . even through 2008!

I was an absolute poster child for: "Stay the course. It will get better." Until 2008, many of us invested our way out of trouble. Between 1963 and 2004, I owned five houses and made great money on every one of them. There were some hiccups in the economy along the way, but my 401(k) and mutual funds recovered quickly. I was also privileged to work at a time when length of service was valued by most companies and encouraged and rewarded.

I was the Senior V. P. of Fortune 500 subsidiary, responsible for 47 sales executives reporting through three regional V.P.'s. The company consistently grew at 15 percent each year and earned 20 percent in operating income. However, the storm clouds were gathering. Our company was a dependable "cash cow" funneling earnings into new ventures and acquisitions that better fit the company strategy of "serving industry's need to know." Their focus was software and acquiring and massaging information to make it valuable to companies. The strategy made sense, but our divorce was painful.

Our company was sold to new owners who replaced the senior management group with its own people, which can happen in these cases. I still have difficulty understanding why all our sales people were fired. These were folks who had an average age of 42, an average length of service of 13 years, and who had established profound and productive relationships with highly positioned customers over a long period of trial and error.

The new owner-strategy perceived that the value of parts of the company exceeded the value of the company as a whole. It was accordingly split into various pieces and sold to the highest bidder . . . quickly.

Long term relationships and their financial value over time were sacrificed for today's profit . . . just like the new financial normal we live with today.

In 1997, I sold our primary residence. Our kids were grown and we didn't need the room or expense of a large home. After capital gains tax and paying off my kids' college debt, I netted about $450,000, which I intended to use to sustain my business and provide some cushion for retirement.

My accountant introduced me to a very successful and well-known broker with a highly regarded firm who put my money in high yield (junk) bonds to keep the business going until it was consistently self-sustaining. After two years, the bonds had lost 40 percent of their value. The yield was fine, but the dramatic shrinkage in the value of the portfolio worried me. In retrospect, there were many things my broker could have done to retain some value of principal, such as replace some of the junk bonds with high-dividend-paying corporate stocks or mutual funds. His parting statement to me was: "You wanted high yield. That's what you got." Because the value of my portfolio was now diminished, I no longer warranted his time and attention, so I was pushed down the line to a less prominent broker in the same, very large and reputable firm. As a result, I pulled the money and put it in C.D.s at 3 percent.

In 2004 we sold our next residence, and after paying off the mortgage and some other debt, I was left with about $300,000. This time I was going to do the investment thinking and my broker would do the execution; I selected a diverse portfolio of large cap, mid—cap and small cap mutual funds from well-known companies. I also bought some emerging market funds, which is exactly what PIMCO's Bill Gross and Warren Buffet would have applauded—a well-diversified mix with a strong performance history, and the safety net of protection from one or more sectors, if another one fails. In 2008 the entire portfolio lost 50 percent of its value. My broker tried to soothe my anguish with this statement: "Consider yourself lucky. Most of my clients lost 60 percent or more. How's the striper fishing on Block Island?"

I pulled the portfolio and bought CDs at 5 percent that quickly started to return only .003 percent. At this point I was withdrawing CD principal every month, which seniors hate to do. I also later determined that some of my small and mid-cap mutual fund money had been invested in World Com, Global Crossings and Enron. In the industry, they call this "style drift," which sometimes happens when a portfolio manager departs from his investment discipline to chase yield. My Reliability-Of-Income alarm was ringing at a very high decibel.

Like many of us, I began to study the new financial normal defining the current investment era in order to determine if financial predictability, and financial certainty, actually existed out there somewhere.

My investigation began with the government's influence on the economy—my investigation accordingly led to little comfort. How can you create confidence in markets with $14.6 trillion in debt and no plan to cut spending? How can you encourage companies to hire when future tax policies could have a substantial negative impact on small business owners who do 70 percent of the hiring?

At the same time, Social Security is in trouble and some changes must be made. At age 73, I'm still working and paying into the system. The retirement age could be increased in a few years, and some means-testing on a limited scale might be in order, and if Bill Gates, Warren Buffet, Ben Stein and others feel an obligation to pay more, we should let them.

On the other hand, most of us started paying into the system early in the program. I started in 1963 and am still paying in today. That's 48 years. If the government had been investing my money instead of spending it, we wouldn't have a problem today, but they followed the Bernie Madoff rules of investment management: Take today's contributions to pay current retirees and hope you draw enough money in the future to keep the scheme alive.

Can we look to the Government for predictability and certainty in our retirement? I don't think so. Part of the new normal in the financial world involves a confusing maze of computers and algorithms, a maze that very few people understand, including many a casino gambler. Last year, many large mutual funds withdrew 40 percent of their monies from their traditional market investments and invested in annuities, gold, real estate and a few carefully selected hedge funds—because even mutual funds are struggling to manage in this era of the so-called "new (financial) normal."

Based on those observations, and after 10 years of experience with investment horror stories, it was time to shed my inflated, Warren Buffet self-image and find a good financial/retirement advisor. No quick fix guy with easy answers but someone who could demonstrate that he had sufficient knowledge, experience, associations, references, proof of long term commitments to clients and, of course, happy clients. I wanted to find someone who would exhibit integrity in taking me through the investment process over time, not someone who would sell me a product today, then move on to someone with deeper pockets tomorrow, at my expense.

The candidate would have to demonstrate that my family would always qualify for enough of his time and mind to offer sage advice through all the financial turmoil the future may have in store for us. This person would have to be emotionally committed to a financial solution that is unique to my circumstances, not a cookie-cutter, one-size-fits-all solution.

My candidate would have to stay ahead of the curve in the ever-changing world of the new normal. I no longer had the time or stomach to revisit the 10-year nightmare I had just endured . . . a financial death delivered through a thousand razor cuts. I intended to take as much time to find such a person as it took for me to extract myself from the many financial messes I was counseled into—by a host of presumed experts who should have known better.

My advisor had to be accessible. I didn't want my phone calls to be retrieved by a voice mail menu asking: "If you want directions to the office press One; for information about financial products press Two." I wanted to be able to speak to my advisor in a reasonable amount of time, any time, and I wanted that conversation to be with him, not a staffer.

Like many of us, the crash of 2008 had an emotional backlash on my family. Like me, they had learned what not to do, who not to trust and had acquired a surprising amount of knowledge about financial products. After my 10-year history of horror, my family would have to be very much involved in my future financial planning, and equally comfortable with my new advisor.

Having learned from experience, and by following the aforementioned rules I set for myself, to locate a good, professional financial/retirement advisor, I suggest that you start by asking a few people you know well and trust who are willing to be honest. We all know plenty of people who were burned in the crash but still can't admit that they didn't see it coming. Avoid these people. They are the same ones who gave you hot stock tips in 2007 that soured; then they accused you of not selling soon enough.

Ask yourself the following questions about your current advisor: How long has this person been your advisor? Does anyone else in your family use him and are they happy with him, and why? How long has he been in business? Have you recommended him to someone else? After some digging, I determined that my ultimate first choice had had his practice for thirteen years and that he had about seven hundred clients.

Three out of four people I questioned mentioned David Reindel, so I focused my evaluation on David Reindel and Reindel Solutions to determine if he would satisfy my advisor-screening criteria.

There were plenty of ways for me to learn more about David Reindel. First, he wrote the book "Don't Die Broke," which had favorable reviews on Amazon. I read the book and found that he had three of my most important criteria: integrity, product knowledge and experience. Also, he is a consistent top performer for Tarkenton Financial and teaches other financial advisors about financial products. In the book, he cited several examples of clients who had problems involving a variety of sums ranging from $20,000 to $20 million, yet each client received his undivided attention and a unique, creative solution—another one of my criteria.

In addition, David conducts about 25 seminars a year to full houses of people interested in retirement planning. I attended a few of these and it was not surprising to see so many people in their 40's and 50's in attendance. I used to think that people who attended these seminars were in diapers and wheel chairs, but not anymore. The impact of the 2008 crash and the reality of having to deal with the new financial normal have brought financial predictability and certainty to top-of-mind with more people. The other appealing aspect of the seminars was David's holistic approach to retirement planning. His subjects included the economy, taxes, probate, legal issues, reverse mortgages, long term care, Medicare, wills and trusts, Social Security, and expense-cutting, along with financial strategies that provide predictability and certainty. In short, there was no product-push. It was all about comprehensive financial management and how each subject differs for different people, based on current financial conditions and family expectations.

These seminars change from time to time, based on the impact of the New Financial Normal. As taxes, government, Social Security, IRA rules, health care, home prices, et cetera, go through their daily spasms, the seminars take a very realistic view of how the important roles of each financial management topic play in cost-containment and Reliability-Of-Income.

David can also be evaluated through his radio program "Don't Die Broke," which aired—at this writing—around southeastern Connecticut on radio station WXLM AM 980 on Sunday mornings, at 10:00 a.m. I listened, later became a client and even a participant on the show, which, in itself, is revealing because most of David's informative guests are actual clients. As I listened to the show, I heard each one share their experience of dealing with the crash of 2008. But again, what I found most telling was that they all came from vastly different financial circumstances and they were all delighted with the way their advisor was managing them into, and through, the retirement process. Unhappy clients don't volunteer to appear and cheerlead on their advisor's radio show.

There was even more exposure of David Reindel through his website called *www.davidreindel.com*, which contains many revealing and interesting topics. Especially revealing are insights about David found through an archive of five to 10-minute segments from the radio show. The segments include comments about every discipline in pre-retirement and post-retirement from guest experts involved in: long term care, probate, reverse mortgage and elder care law, bond and stock investing, taxes and government—which is still important to me because the crash of 2008 proved that all these disciplines can play a role in our future financial predictability and certainty, not just a financial product.

I have also learned to look at customer focus. Many companies promote this quality in their mission statements. They have endless meetings with advertising agencies, P.R. firms and human resource experts to determine the many ways to promote customer service. Yet, very few deliver. In spite of their best intentions, they become distracted with legal, marketing, regulatory or employee issues. Their best intentions for customer focus tend to fade away as a result.

I found that the Reindel business model delivers on customer focus and customer service. That's how he can handle 700 clients seamlessly. I have been a client for a number of years and I'm always made to feel that I'm the only client he has. He works this miracle by outsourcing everything that interferes with his interface with the customer, so the distractions that are trappings to so many others in his business do not ensnare him.

After looking at many candidates, only David Reindel passed through all of my check points. I set the first appointment and, over time, made five more appointments. We covered my financials, expenses, income and expectations; we brought the family into the meetings, and we all looked into various options. I was put in charge of managing my own financial future while David provided the input for risk/reward ratios and some unique, creative financial thinking. He provided all the pieces to the financial mosaic, and with his guidance, I carefully put them in place.

My Solution: I bought a "fixed index annuity" and looking back on the decision, I'm happy about it. The annuity delivers everything that can be delivered with predictability and certainty. My annuity guarantees a 6 percent return for income each year from a highly regarded and well capitalized insurance company—insurance companies are required by law to maintain sufficient reserves to cover their financial commitments. Also, I can withdraw the cash each year or, if my business has a good year, the 6 percent yield is added to my principle. Additionally, I can withdraw up to 20 percent of the principle each year without penalty, in case we have a major emergency. My fixed index annuity also has a "kicker," which means that a small amount of my principal is applied to the S&P 500 Index each year. If the Index gains at the end of the year, the gain is added to my principal. If the Index loses, my benchmark returns to my starting number from the beginning of each investment year. So I loose nothing. In my judgment, there is no Reliability-Of-Income investment that provides predictability and certainty with better returns than this.

If someday I am able to accumulate enough to jump back into the "return-on-investment" world, instead of the reliability of income world, I may try double shorts on treasuries, the volatility index, or my favorite, which is called "the strangle." But that's another strategy for another time to come.

As for today, those of us who have survived the crash are now being inundated with T.V. commercials from the same financial giants who were unable to stop our financial bleeding while they were in charge of our assets. We are now getting advice from the same people saying: "Trust us. You need a partner you can depend on. You can count on us to secure your future." Their stories of financial strength, integrity and promises of a secure future fall on deaf ears. Billions of dollars have been withdrawn from stock and bond mutual funds from demoralized investors who followed the advice of these same, admired and well-established financial giants who failed them. Their customers won't be back soon. Loyalty must be earned again, over time.

Knowledge, experience and associations that these financial giants promote are only valuable to you and me if they accompany a passionate commitment to the customer.

I am 74 years old. Over the years, I have retained the services of 21 advisors from many disciplines: insurance (some of my friends and relatives are in the business), stock brokers (two huge public companies with advisors loaded with certifications), accountants, real estate brokers, bankers and lawyers.

From twenty one advisors, I would select only three who put my best interest ahead of their own personal gain: one banker, one real estate broker and David Reindel. They are all very successful because they follow the same basic philosophy: "If I take care of my customer, the money will take care of itself."

Because I chose to work closely with these individuals, for now I sleep well, and I sincerely wish all of you the same.

#

CHAPTER 14

Parting Comments about
Fixed Indexed Annuities

From David Reindel

What is the *fixed index annuity* definition of R.O.I.? If you're thinking "return on investment," think again. We call it "Reliability of Income."

As of June 30, 2010, fixed index annuities were up $168 billion and they continued to grow through the following year, as well. People are flocking to safe havens and before you ask what is, or isn't, a safe haven, let me guide the way.

Sometimes in the past when I uttered the word "annuity," people just recoiled, but it's a word that we're going to have to get used to hearing. Annuities were designed from the beginning of time, from the days of ancient Rome, to provide income. The Romans invented the term *annuity*—that's where the word comes from—yet, in our modern day society, the income planning we can do with the annuity is far more flexible and offers much more certainty with income riders.

We're also looking at the potential of some annuities to be offered for the 401(k). I think that within five years or so, people who are building up their retirements will have this as an option, as do people in retirement right now.

But you have to understand annuities and you have to understand *the one that works for you*. I haven't done any actual planning in this book because everyone is individual. Instead, I've let others show you their plans with the caution that their situations would probably not work for you. This is because you and your situation will be entirely different. I can almost guarantee it.

Do you have qualified money or non-qualified money, after-tax money or before-tax money? And how much do you have? I use a laddering system I call the Income Planner, which I'm using for somebody, right now, to utilize tax and income savings.

Since the days of yore (meaning a few days before the '08 crash), the financial press has improved a bit here and there, when covering annuities, but some of them still don't understand what they're talking about. For them, and for anyone interested in learning more from a factual source, a source not affiliated with any particular annuity company or product representative, go to the web site run by the National Association of Fixed Annuities (NAFA), where you will find information to counter any lingering, misinformed news reports. Keep in mind that NAFA is an industry lobbying group for annuity producers and carriers; we have to lobby in Congress for better tax breaks for annuities and we have to work through NAFA to counter unfriendly press coverage now and then.

But if you have any doubts about annuities after reading this book—or after reading my previous book, *Don't Die Broke*—let's look at the prevailing media game, based on a 2010 article in the *Wall Street Journal*. The article claimed to set the record straight in a story called "The Downside of Downside Protection," which ran against bold facts we all have right in front of us.

In the story, the *WSJ* states that "the insurer promises to pay a minimum income of 1 percent to 3 percent" in apparently all annuities, as if those figures were set in stone for the entire industry. If you have learned anything about annuities by now, you know that rates of income are all over the map. I have a fixed index annuity that pays 6 percent for income purposes.

Today, in the context of income planning, we have a build-up account on the index side for the accumulation of earnings, and we have and a guaranteed account to be used for income purposes, for someone wanting income right away based on 6 percent accumulation per year.

For those wanting to take advantage of tax deferral for a period of time, we use a 6 percent earnings model. Using different formulas, we try to find the one that fits your situation, and this kind of strategy has recently been offered with certain variable annuities as well. In fact, the once notorious variable annuity typically offers an income rider to provide more certainty of knowing what the income level would be.

With the index annuity, we certainly don't know what kind of earnings we're going to get from year to year, but we have downside protection. Unlike the variable annuity, index annuities guarantee against the loss of your principal when the market goes down. But in the WSJ article they talk about little more than the index annuity's limitation on upside earnings, without a word about the fact that you will not lose a dime on the downside. Of course annuity carriers have to limit upside gains! They have to do this to protect your money against the loss of accumulated principal in downside markets, like the market after the Crash of 2008.

The *WSJ* goes on to say that "the insurer links a minor additional amount to the S&P 500 index, or some other option, and you get a slice of any gains . . . and no losses." That's more like it. I don't take issue with that. Fact is, my own clients, on average over 12 years, have received between 3 percent and 7.58 percent gains, depending on when they started, and according to market conditions during the period. But nobody has lost principal.

As if to make this product sound negative, the *WSJ* went on to note that, " . . . these products normally have a cap of 6 percent, which is the excess you can pick up over and above your guarantee, so if the S&P 500 gets 8 percent or 10 percent, you only get 6 percent." And . . . ? My point is SO WHAT? You still get a 6 percent gain without having to worry about the downside loss of principal. That . . . is . . . the . . . WHOLE POINT! That's the key. The mathematical truth is that you will not lose principal, yet you stand to participate in SOME of the gain in an up market. What could be better than that?

Ironically, I've seen ads in the *Wall Street Journal* run by certain insurance companies that actually show the same figures in charts, for everyone to see. Again, if you sit down with me I'll show you the math. A Wharton School of Business study is perhaps a more reliable source, given that Wharton is one of the most reputable business schools in the country. The Wharton study, which I can send to you, was conducted over a period of 12 years, and it specifically mentions the same problems with press coverage that we've seen in recent years.

The important thing, in my opinion, is that the journalist who wrote the story is focused on the idea that you might see 3 percent earnings from your total contribution for a period of time, rather than the fact that your substantial balance is guaranteed. As if anybody who has ever been in the market over a period of time doesn't already know: Losses, either sporadic or prolonged, can be devastating.

I see clients every day that had assets in the $300ks drop to the $200ks, and if they continue in the market, I think they stand a good chance of dying broke. As an alternative, we're applying money with guaranteed-income planning in mind, something our critics don't seem to understand. They don't seem to hear when people like me, when I plainly state: The only reason I think you should have an annuity is for income purposes. Income is the only reason. It's not there for your heirs, it's for you, but if something is left over in your annuity—as opposed to your Social Security account—your heirs will get it.

So many articles in mainstream business journalism dwell on ROI as a "return-on-investment. As if risk will never again lead to loss, they go on week after week about how to time the market—often a disaster for amateur investors—or, how to take advantage of volatility, in and out strategies, that kind of thing. True to the typical, the positive perspective our *WSJ* journalist brings to the article is based on a return-on-investment strategy, as opposed to Reliability of Income. This is a major difference of philosophy, of course, which should be presented as a matter of choice, not an ultimatum favoring risk. Yet, I also notice that many an author of such articles will tend to be fairly young, therefore able to relate to a younger perspective based on gain, loss and eventual recovery, over time. Unfortunately, many of us no longer have that kind of luxury.

If I have adequate income, I have pension, I have Social Security. If I have enough income and I don't need the money, then I can see having some risk of principal. But despite articles like the one above, people are becoming more conservative. They're leaving the market in droves.

When somebody comes into my office, I ask how much they want to protect. Almost to the last person, they will say they want to protect ALL of it. Nobody says, "HALF of it," or "a LITTLE bit." They say, "ALL OF IT." So, in tune with the times, we're looking at strategies that provide that kind of protection. After all, we tend to insure our homes and cars, why not our money? And if you want to accomplish that, you have to sit down with a competent planner like myself, look at the math, and understand what this particular scenario means for you.

I know it's a major learning curve. There was a period of time when a mutual fund would appreciate, seemingly with no end in sight. We all enjoyed years and years when our homes were appreciating at the rate of 6, 7, even 10 percent or more per year. But that was when unethically leveraged loans were artificially hyping the housing market, and that is no longer the case. As a result of prior markets, we have years of foreclosure inventory to absorb before we see substantial gains again. In spite of all that, people still want no risk and a 100 percent return, but you can't get that.

In the end, you will eventually find that protection of principal and guaranteed income must be in place before you take additional risk. But don't take my word for it. If you still have doubts, go back and review the profiles of the real people in this book.

In this book, I think you will have discovered a pattern, and that pattern will become an essential part of the New Normal in the years to come.

The New Financial Normal: Let's Talk Solutions

On that note, we're talking about retirement "income" dollars, as opposed to "investment" dollars, which represent an entirely different arena—and that's not what we're talking about here.

When dealing with income dollars earned with annuities, you also face surrender charges for early withdrawal, which raise media criticism every time the subject come up.

Let's talk about surrender charges, what some people call the "white flag, I give up, throw in the towel" moment of abandonment.

The reality is that surrender charges have steadily improved through the years, and states have levied a lot more regulation over surrender charges. For one thing, if you're hearing about 20-year surrender periods and 20 percent surrender charges, those are in annuities I never use, and they're on the way out, in my opinion. Such charges may not make sense to you but surrender charges in general have an important function. The concept of the surrender charge is this: You make a commitment and the company makes a commitment; then you stick with it, depending on your situation, for a period of typically five or 10 years. These days, however, some products even have a complete Return of Premium rider that allows you to get your money back anytime you want.

The annuity owned by Richard (featured in the last chapter) lets him take up to 10 percent of the total contribution to his annuity the first year, and 10 percent the second year, without any surrender charge. So, this is not your grandfather's annuity, but you must understand how it's going to work for you and how you're going to use it. For example, don't plan to use the retirement income dollars in your annuity to go out and buy a car, or to pay off your kid's college debt. You want to preserve your annuity income dollars in a secure place that will stay in place for a long time.

No doubt, the surrender charge and the need for commitment to annuity stipulations represent a big topic. You need to understand exactly how they work, and you need to be aware of the new innovations available because NOT ALL annuities carry huge surrender charges or lengthy surrender periods. This is a myth certain media outlets would love to have you believe. Well, don't believe it.

Meanwhile, we just saw the end of a power struggle that would have placed annuities under the control of the Securities Exchange Commission, which obviously favors investment in, and regulation of, securities. Behind the scenes, the SEC wanted to take control of annuities away from the states and put them under federal government jurisdiction, among other things. But it doesn't look like that's going to happen and we're glad to hear it. I think that my state understands the effect annuities have on its own people far more intimately than would a roomful of Washington bureaucrats, and I also think that annuities should be offered by people who best understand annuities, as opposed to people who favor and better understand securities, although both should have the ability to offer annuities. After all, what better time would there be for a securities broker to offer some client safety in annuities—if we face another market crash, if all the signs were pointing to another catastrophic downturn? I'm all for brokers who offer annuities along with whatever else they do in the market.

A good friend of mine in his mid-50s said he has been beaten up badly in the stock market. Not once but twice. He could have paid his kid's college education twice, but instead he lost it all twice, and he's obviously upset about it.

He did look at annuities and asked me how much, according to his age, I thought he should set aside as retirement income in annuities. Given the new normal he asked, more specifically, how old he *should have been* when locking into retirement income, and stringing barbed wire around the package to protect it.

We can't go back in time for this client, so I won't go there. We have to start where we are and move forward. If he's in his 50s, we have to look at what he's going to have available when he reaches retirement. So, first we look for things like a pension and how much would be available from Social Security. Then we back into the numbers because what we want to provide—with income annuities—are the dollars to fill the gaps for expenses, and, in his case, no more. That's how we'd do it in one scenario. It's an income planning process. It takes many meetings. I have people coming in and out of the office until they come up with a realistic budget, as with one client, in particular, who came up with a final budget that literally doubled after our first meeting.

When we're done—on that very day—we know how much money is going to be there, period. That's retirement income planning. That's what it is all about.

I trust that you have been able to glean some useful information from the pages of this book, more specifically from the real people who were kind enough to donate their time—and some very personal stories—in order to illustrate the critical value of income planning.

Obviously, guaranteed-income planning has been a passion for me for many years, and it has become ultimately satisfying since the unseen ravages of the Great Recession brought new focus to the concepts I've been passing on to my clients all along. If some of those concepts appeal to you, please don't hesitate. Make the move to ensure some guaranteed principal and income for yourself. Know the reality of *peace of mind* for what it is: a truly precious treasure!

That said, after a few concluding comments of my own, I would like to pass the baton to my good friend, Fran Tarkenton, as he delivers superb wisdoms in the final epilogue of this book.

—*David Reindel*

#

CHAPTER 15

Parting Comments from Dave and Fran Tarkenton

ABOUT MY NEXT GUEST AND HIS FINAL WORDS OF WISDOM

We all know that Fran Tarkenton was a great NFL quarterback. But for most of his life, Fran has been even better known across America for his wonderful skills related to the creation of successful businesses of all kinds.

I called Fran about seven years ago when he was starting Tarkenton Financial because I was looking for somebody who is as passionate about his business as I am about mine. I knew from research that Fran is a dedicated businessman with keen insights into what people really need to get the job done. In this case, it's the process of getting retirees into a solid and safe path of income.

Fran invited me down to Atlanta, he laid out the direction he planned for Tarkenton Financial and it paralleled the road I was on. So, I decided to join up with Fran and we've since become business partners and good friends.

That's why he wrote the foreword to my last book. Now he has been generous enough to write the parting epilogue for this one.

Fran is a great business man and he believes in safe places for money. During the early years of our relationship, he told me about some friends of his who were losing money, were not able to retire, were having to go back to work and they knew there had to be some answers out there.

As Fran learned more about annuities, he came to understand that they are designed for guaranteed income. The annuity is the only thing on the planet that will do that for you. They were designed for that in the beginning, they're better today, and there's so much more innovation: For example, there are guaranteed income riders and the list of newly available features keeps on growing. They are far from being your grandfather's annuity.

Yet, as I've been saying throughout this book, if you have one, it should be for income. Fran and I put annuities into retirement portfolios for income purposes because they're great tools for just that purpose. And if you don't use up all the income in your annuity, it can go to your heirs, unlike Social Security for example, which I can start receiving at 62. But, again, when I die my Social Security checks die with me. With an annuity, all that income goes to my heirs.

Fran and I always talk about one thing: Too many people fail to understand what they have, where they're going, or why. That's typical, they don't have a plan. Fran says, "An idiot with a plan is better than a genius with no plan." But if you have a plan, it's not just about the plan, it's about everything around the plan including beneficiaries, long-term care, intended purposes for the money in the plan, and so forth.

When you take the initiative and sit down with somebody and start making a plan, you take control of your own destiny from that point forward. But first, you need to separate investments versus money set aside for retirement.

Retirement money should be for retirement purposes. It should be for the Reliability of Income we've talked about in previous chapters. Unfortunately, most people don't get that far because they never really develop a strategy. They just invest money and hope that when they're ready to retire, there will be enough to live on.

My last book, titled Don't Die Broke, just happened to come out when the crash of 2008 began to happen, so I can take some credit for helping to save some retirement portfolios among my readers. But after the crash, people everywhere really began looking at annuities. Since the book came out and after the crash, I've seen interest from some people who were totally market-oriented before. They come to me saying, "I have to take something off the table, I have to have some guaranteed income." I say, "I can do that," and I do.

With the tools we have available today, I can tell you at the age of 60 what your income will be at 66.

It's all about Reliability of Income and ROI works like this: If you're taking income from a stock portfolio—say you have a $500,000 portfolio and you're taking 5 percent income—if that portfolio goes to $300,000, you have to either decrease your income or you have to hope and pray that it's going to come back. We know markets are cyclical. They're always going up and down, up and down, but what if your equity losses don't come back before you pass away, or before you grow too old to enjoy them? You go broke, that's what.

Can 2008 happen again? Yes, it can. If you're scared to death, or justly and wisely afraid of losing money in the market, now is the time to make an income decision, not when accounts are down and you find yourself working from fear.

Mutual funds were smacked so badly during the last decade because their managers did not have safe solutions built into their strategies. But today, I'm more concerned about "flash-crash" deflation, uncertainty, taking mutual funds into safe haven and more, and annuities are part of the solution. We don't have all the answers but we have reliable ideas about how to provide income and it's worth a look.

So, have an open mind and avoid "confirmation bias," which, again, is how we shut out new information about things we don't understand. The result can be disastrous.

We're in a great moment right now and it's time to make decisions. People have been getting out of the market and running, since 2008, toward making the kinds of retirement decisions that will ensure their financial safety in the face of things to come, which Fran will explain in the following, conclusive commentary.

Meanwhile, I hope you have been able to benefit from the real-life stories in this book. For me, it's time to put down the pen and get back to work for my clients.

Until we meet again, either on the air, through our web site or even in my office, the very best to you, and above all,

Happy Planning!

David Reindel
Reindel Advisory Solutions,
Mystic, Connecticut

From here into the future, I wish you the best. Take heart and take care,

—David Reindel

#

Final Wisdoms and a Warning
By Fran Tarkenton

I did play football in the National Football League for 18 years, but for most of my life I've been a serial entrepreneur and I've built a lot of businesses. One of them is a business based in Atlanta, Ga., called Tarkenton Financial, where we work with people to look at their retirement income planning, and we have a couple hundred financial advisors across the country.

That's all we do: work with people on their retirement planning, and one of our advisors is Dave Reindel. He is probably the most knowledgeable guy in this business. His ethics are impeccable. He has worked with so many people, putting together responsible retirement income planning and they have profited from what he has told them.

Not long ago, he decided to do another book. Although I thought *Don't Die Broke* was one of the best, most essential, books on retirement planning that I have ever read, I was a little skeptical about this one because books are books are books. He wrote this book and the title is pretty significant in this day and time because it talks about the way real people survived the horrific Crash of 2008. You have discovered their stories in this most compelling new book.

In it, you have seen first-hand information from the very people who survived, using our principles based on guaranteed income and safety of principal, which I know will be absolutely essential in the coming years.

In these pages, you have seen the living truth about the way people lost huge amounts of their retirement savings. But they were able to bounce back with Dave's strategies. What additional proof do we need that his concepts are a must in this troubled global economy?

This is not only a great book, it's a book that addresses the truth about retirement after the 2008 crash. It's a book you want your friends and family members to read at a time when most of us have learned tough lessons about financial calamity—in a financial situation that we never thought we'd see in this country.

It is a sad fact that we have finally gotten to the point that we don't know what to believe or who to trust. Well, Dave Reindel is one person you need to believe; he's one you can trust. I've worked with him for a number of years and he is as good as it gets. So, if you have any doubt about the value of the advice you have seen in this book, doubt no more.

After visiting with Dave, I asked him why he wrote this book and he told me that he'd seen a lot of people come to his practice since the crash. They were upset, worried, downright scared, but one of his goals was to get them to think differently when they retire. He pointed out that many of them had been living off their assets, not really doing anything differently and hoping for the same results. He saw that people had been losing income power, basically guessing about income.

Can you blame them? All we ever knew was to listen to stock brokers talk about safe stocks and that the banks were safe, and that General Motors and Chrysler and Ford were safe, and that's all we knew. Then Dave told us the truth: that we've gotten to a point in this country where we're morphing into investing for retirement instead of saving for retirement. There can be no certainty with investments in General Motors stock, Ford stock. There is no certainty in dividends today. We've come into a different world.

The world I knew was changing as I was reading his last book and I cannot believe how prophetic it has become. Since then, people all over America have started planning for retirement using certainty, and one of the vehicles that we have for certainty is the annuity. These instruments are about guaranteeing and protecting—essentially insuring—your money. Today, that's what we do.

Dave tells us that annuities are an insurance product, and he's dead-on. Insurance companies sell annuities and Dave makes a good point when he says that we insure our houses and cars, so why not insure our retirement money, too?

Why not insure your income in retirement? After all, with annuities, your principal is not at risk. So, why not provide for some insured income with your annuity?

Since the crash, people have changed. We used to talk about getting into annuities when we were in our 50s and 60s, but now we see people in their 40s who start looking at annuities, too, because they're already looking for a safe-retirement horizon, and they start wondering—right then—what they should do to ensure safety in retirement.

Think about it. Dave always says you "shouldn't be guessing about your retirement when you can PLAN it." I agree: You shouldn't be guessing but that's exactly what we do when we bet our retirement assets on the stock market. There are so many people who *still* guess. They look at the "what-ifs." They look at belief. If you believe that General Motors stock is going up you're going to buy it, right? If you believe it's going to go down, you're not going to buy it, right? Well, Dave notes that with insurance products there is absolutely NO belief required because, if you do *this*, then *that* will happen. And *that* is exactly what the term "insurance" implies. If you follow the rules built into an insurance product like the annuity, the results *will surely be* what you expect.

So, you can certainly plan your retirement with greater certainty, which reminds me of my favorite quotes. You've already seen it in this book but I'll say it again: "An idiot with a plan will always beat a genius with no plan." What Dave tried to do in his first book was to put together all the ideas and plans he's been using over the years, in order to help people plan for income and save their retirement in the process.

In this book, he shows you, through real life examples of living people, just how incredibly critical his kind of strategy became, both before and after the Crash of 2008 came down. Because of the strategies put in place by Dave Reindel, and similar strategies used by the rest of us at Tarkenton Financial, the key word in the title of this book was entirely possible: Dave's clients "Survived."

His clients, the people in this book, can safely say "*We Survived the Crash*" because it's true, which makes it such a powerful title.

Since you've now read this book to the end, either pass it on or call up everyone you know and get them to go out and buy a copy. Everybody who's 45 or over should read this book. Tell them to get it from any retailer or online bookstore like Amazon.com, or they can get it from Dave's web site: *www.davidreindel.com*. But whatever you do, just tell them to get it.

The information in this book is not only essential, it is the foundation that drove the people in it to "survive the crash," hence the title. If you now understand Dave's life-saving, retirement preserving concepts, you also know they work through real-live results in action, from real people who listened to Dave and put his knowledge to practice.

These people, the real people in this book, tell their stories in a way that anyone can understand. They are not retirement experts or stock market wizards. They are just good, hard-working people who did everything they could to save for retirement.

Some of them got caught up in the stock market crash in 2008 and lost. But even then, Dave was able to go in and help them take what they had left and, this time around, preserve their principal and set up guaranteed income for the rest of their lives.

That's the power of this book. You hear it straight from the people who have lived it and it doesn't get any better than that. I think, if you're like me, you've found yourself somewhere in this book and I think you've discovered good reasons to take the same road. If you do, you will thank yourself because ONE DAY, the same kind of horrible crash that wiped out so many retirement plans will happen again.

That's no gamble. That's no bet. That is what will happen, and you can count on it. So, take the concepts in "We Survived the Crash" to heart and you won't die broke. That I can guarantee.

Most Sincerely,

Fran Tarkenton.

*   *   *

ACKNOWLEDGEMENTS

From the Editor's Desk

After reading this book, be sure to get a copy of "Don't Die Broke," which has been selling nationwide to a growing audience of both average and highly sophisticated investors looking for safety in our previous and current economic climate, all of whom have discovered the vital need for reliable income for the future.

Know that all of the people profiled in this book are real clients of Dave Reindel and that each one volunteered his or her information without coercion, payment or other forms of reimbursement of any kind. Thus, their comments are their own. They were not scripted or prompted. They came from one-on-one interviews and their comments about David Reindel come from direct experience and are unbiased. As such, not all clients profiled here are entirely invested in annuities or in any other products recommended by David Reindel or Reindel Advisory Solutions. Many of these clients are, in fact, quite independent in their thinking, having chosen to make their own decisions regarding investments including equities, bonds, real estate and other alternatives.

The principals at Reindel Advisory Solutions are proud of the above. They are in the business of making sure that no one will "die broke" or fail to "survive the crash" when the next one comes around. They also wish to point out that no specific recommendations or solicitations have been made for any particular annuity or investment product from any specific annuity carrier. This is because such products are in constant flux. Annuities and their applicability to specific situations are subject to constant change.

As always, consult a highly qualified professional before purchasing any annuity. As with any financial product, you should consider consulting a CPA for tax planning purposes, and the appropriate type of attorney when certain estate management issues arise.

That said, thank you for reading *"We Survived the Crash."* We hope it will make a difference in your life, wherever your planning strategies may take you in the future, which, as they say, will eventually become the all-encompassing *now*.

Yours Very Truly,

The Editor

\#

CPSIA information can be obtained at www.ICGtesting.com
Printed in the USA
BVOW071152300512

291335BV00002B/3/P